Joyful Walking

Dear Rachael

Enjoy those walks!

Love Iain Dryden.

Joyful Walking

Reaping life's wonders

Iain Dryden

With the author's sketches from walks around the world

CONTENTS

Dedicated to you who walk.

Each of these pages is a gossamer strand of a rescue blanket.
Slipped over your daily life, this fine shawl silently transmutes an
ordinary existence into something quite special, quite worthwhile.
Your supposedly dull life becomes special, each moment a
treasure.
You float out of bed and the day which once yawned before you
becomes a living wonder.

INTRODUCTION

There is walking... and there is springing beyond the ordinary. In the latter, we step out vibrant and at home with ourselves, even as we stride off to work. However, most of us shuffle along mildly disgruntled. This is not our fault, life stresses us on so many levels. It doesn't have to be like this, after all our distant cousins, today's foraging or herding tribes, are generally healthier and happier.

Don't beat yourself up, science shows us the way back. You are the centre of your world, everything you do is tinted by your view of yourself. Imagine the soothing effect of being utterly comfortable with a self unspoilt by ego games. Composed, you'd enjoy your environment, relish the moment. This is achievable, this little book shows you how.

After a barrage of diseases ruined my once bounteous health, permanently encumbered, I sought an easy, research based way to improve my well-being. I discovered that self-compassion is the best way to reduce stress and energise our weary minds. That sounds woolly, confusing, but we get there by respecting the extraordinary body and mind we inhabit - three billion years of experimentation and innovation are manifest in you!

Walking, a fun and restorative activity, seemed the obvious vehicle; as these sketches show, until recently, I have walked great distances all my life. When you walk, channel your natural attributes by employing the effortless exercises in this book. Slip these concise actions into your daily routine, at home, at work, and gradually construct a powerful new mindset, a secure cognitive stillness.

Skip into the fresh air observant of the changing scenery, alert to serendipity. A humdrum walk becomes a mini adventure, even the traffic's roar turns into an orchestral rumble. When you are fully engrossed, your walks become your mentor, and the sparkle slips into your ordinary existence.

The key is to see that we can tweak our characters ! You have to really want to change for it to happen… and being consistent is vital. You can't hurry this joyous journey - patience, enjoyment and smiling at oneself are essential if you wish to get the most from these pages.

Using Joyful Walking

Get the most from this book by relishing *one* page at a time, slowly absorbing the information. Give yourself 2-3 months to complete the processes, or nothing lasting will occur. Allow the **micro-boost** exercises **(in bold)** to augment your walks. You'll gradually condense these to 30 second bursts, transforming your walking experience and much, much more….

COBBLES

About seven million years ago a group of apes split from their ancestors. Over time, by trial and error they evolved a new diet and complex social interactions which necessitated developing grammatical language. This provoked imagination and the abstract thought required for problem solving, they exploited fire and created sophisticated tools. Hey presto - your ancestors!

Take the act of walking as an example. You would have prepared yourself by comparing one path against another, by thinking of things you might encounter, such as traffic volume or minor dangers. This involves breathtaking mental gymnastics, yet it seems normal. However, being tech savvy wonders we think we've hit the sweet spot, though we've missed it. We are so enamoured by our minds' acrobatics that we are less conscious of our pre-human brains, consequently, as we walk we are hardly aware of where our feet land. Acute awareness of our astounding physiological history enhances our walks, this can be done by developing a mindset poised (so as to speak) between the 'human' and 'animal' brain. Lingering 'there', we discover we are greater than the peculiar character we've been taught to think of as 'Me'. Allow these pages to take you 'there' one stride at a time, make each walk special as you discover your incredible heritage. Now for our first *micro-boost*.

Notice your shifting weight sinking into your shoes, your ankles adjusting with the angle of the path, your breath changing. Be aware of the ground you pass over... perhaps the change from tar to cobbles, the slightly uneven paving or the softness of the soil. Flit back and forth from your mental ramblings to your body and the world it is rambling through - savour being *you*, and tell yourself, "What a treat!"

Spilling down to a tiny fishing harbour, alluring Clovelly is astride the South West Coastal Path - 630 miles of largely unspoilt scenery skirting Devon, Cornwall and Dorset. Clovelly, Devon, England.

ⓐ

STONE

Bend down, pick up a stone and as you walk, relish it.

Our relationship with stone is profound for it is one of the factors which defines our species. Apes throw stones at attackers, they use them to crack nuts, and upon Kenya's fertile plains we humans invented the Swiss Army knife 2.6 million years before Switzerland came into being. With our stone tools we sliced food, made hard points for our spears, in countless ways stone implements improved our existence, helping to grow our brains. No wonder pebbles and stone circles are appealing.

Grasp your stone and sink into your physical form, feeling yourself not as you but as a human figure alone in the rawness of nature and know this stone is your pal. As is your vigilance, for at root we still have the raw alertness of our Stone Age ancestors. Dig a little deeper and you notice you are also prehuman. Your inner most brain, a vigorous kernel atop the spine, is the instinctual reptilian* brain. This is capped by an emotional mammalian* brain. Surrounding these is the neocortex, ape* brain; it is fronted by humanity's outstanding prefrontal cortex.

Linger for a while and explore the stone's attributes, sensing its temperature, its firmness; is it textured, dented, heavy? Enjoy your lizard senses, ape feelings and human thoughts weaving together, making you you.

---

* Popular, not scientific, terms.

Two walkers passed
behind me, one complained he'd
like a chair like mine to sit on. The other
said it was only a mile to their hotel now. And
suddenly the sun came out to light this
ancient gateway. Then the cold got in
to my fingers and I
retreated

e is a magic to Dartmoor.
ines from the lichen clad walls.
lluminates the spaces between objects,
lips silently into your mind.

Astride Devon's fertile ridges, Dartmoor, with its 160 tors, 5,090 ancient stone rows, stone circles and stone-hut remains, is enchanted by many tales which enrich the walker's day. Devon, England.

STEP

We ought to thank our little feet all the time, yet we ignore them as they carry us here and there. No longer needing to climb trees, natural selection gradually favoured those of our ancestors whose feet became more rigid.

Stop walking, lift your ankles high, drop them, again and again. Now rock from foot to foot. Notice how your toes work to keep you upright. What a refined instrument you keep stamping on!

In each foot twenty six bones move thirty three joints, with over one hundred muscles, tendons and ligaments arranged in three interacting arches - inner, outer and transverse. These arches stretch and flex as you roll forward, transferring weight to your toes. This elasticity absorbs energy. As you lift off the ground the tendons snap, exploding that stored power to each step. This adds lightness to your fabulous human foot.

Slow your walking pace from time to time and appreciate the movement of this staggering architecture which makes moving more efficient. Imagine a splay of thick rubber bands stretching from your toes to your heel and releasing power as you move.

A cobbler returning the spring to my shoes after 6 weeks non-stop trekking. Kumoan Himalaya, India.

HUES

Upon today's walk, stop and breath in deeply as you stretch your arms high and out. Hold. Hold. Hold. Let it out slowly. Don't worry, others will assume this is joy manifest after a decent walk.

Scan the scene before you. How many colours can you count in the *left* quarter? Select one, how many subtle hues of this colour can you detect? If there's a large expanse of it, are there changes from density to lightness?

Shift your eyes to the *right* quarter. Can you find the same colour? Do the same discriminatory exercise. Compare the differences between these shades and those you saw a moment ago. It is the changing light from one spot to another which creates the many hues. **Briefly admire a puff of trees, the rocks or bricks in a wall, reflections in puddles or windows.**

Quantifying your environment isn't only a mental distraction, it illuminates your slog to work for it energises the brain. This simple, proven visual exercise helps those who suffer from anxiety or depression. It is more effective than it might seem, over time it will brighten the quality of your outlook.

Bared to simple hues, the market square, Limoux, Aude, France.

ⓐ
TENSION

With time enough to cover the distance, you find your lively little feet hurrying along, pacing across your precious distance as if it did not matter. Why, when there's no need to hurry? Because stresses and strains inside you are welling up and your body responds as if you are being chased by a tiger.

It isn't easy to slow those tiny toes. Tightness in your lungs, tension in your neck, a light headache behind your temples, a mild strain in your eyes. These things propel you forwards, for your body knows tiger's claws are sharp.

STOP!
remember there's no tiger-danger.

Take a deep breath ... feel the tension in your chest, belly and back; tighten them all. Let it out very slowly as you relax. Repeat this no more than six times.

Look at anything, a stone, an ant, a leaf, a cloud. Notice its form, how the light catches various parts, admire it for being what it is. The magic in simple stuff!

Breathe in, do a little jump, letting air out as you land. Jig them feet, un-tensing those tigers and chuckle! Sheer madness. Our time is short and it is ours to dance with.

Sheltering under the ivy from a torrent

Tense, tired, still a long way to go, but finding relaxation in a downpour when rounding the Cherbourg peninsular, France.

ⓐ
BREATHING

You might not think it as you puff up hill, but breathing is a graceful process. The involuntary nervous system instructs the lungs to enlarge, creating low pressure and air is subsequently sucked in. This heats up and expands, forcing us to expel air 17,000 times a day. Inside your lungs, minute alveoli transfer the oxygen content to your veins. Red blood cells then carry it all over your body, retaining 5% whilst your cells expel waste CO_2.

When we are stressed we breathe badly, and as most of us are always mildly on edge, our breathing is all-a-kilter. A rasping breath arises with disturbed emotion, as does a racing heart, so breathing slowly **fully in and fully out six times** (go on, do it), eases the nervous system, setting off a reaction which dissipates the stress chemical cortisol. Women giving birth are encouraged to attentively **breathe deeply and slowly°.** Some doctors promote breathing exercises, the Army does too, so why not you?

Painfully over-puffing up that hill? Slowing your pace combined with gentle, rhythmic deep breathing relaxes the body and lessens pain's grip on the mind. Habitual mountain walkers already know fluid breathing is vital.

Go on, try it.

Do read this -
  https://www.ncbi.nlm.nih.gov/pubmed/21939499

° Explained a little more fully in my book 'Settling"

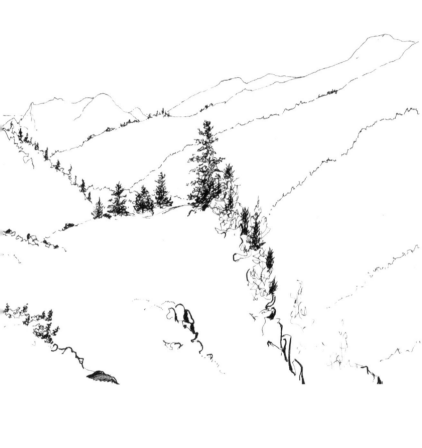

Rippling Himalayan slopes made lugging my heavy pack hard from those distant North Indian Plains where I'd started walking ten days before.

SUN

Ah, the warmth of the summer's first sunburst! As we walk our skin feels alive, our mind brightens, our spirits lift. We need the sun's vitamin D and after a winter wrapped in clothes, what a boost.

Take off your shoes, recline and bathe your hard working feet in sunlight. Close your eyes, feel the heat touching your toes, seeping in to the top of your foot, relaxing your ankles. Feel this warmth spreading up your legs and into your entire body.

We who enjoy the benefits of electrical power on tap take for granted that vast object in the sky which ignites our days, yet humanity has exalted the sun for millennia. Across India's enormity, each sunrise and sunset people still sing the sun ritual hymn, reminding themselves that we owe our very existence to this glorious globe. Without the sun, planet Earth would be iced up, with it, our magnificent orb thrives.

At sunset allow your fleeting mind to delight in a drama performed for the dinosaurs. Stand tall, admire in great detail every hue and feeling and emotion created by the greatest light show on Earth. Know this is a performance for you alone, for on that path across the valley it'll look and feel slightly different. Ha! The pleasure of being alive right here. Close your eyes, 'see-feel' the sun on your forehead; sink into this delicious sensation.

The sun's splendour renders us insignificant, it signifies our fragility.

Carrying rice and spices to Mattancherry.

Spice laden boats in the dawn sunlight cross paths with fishermen's canoes before old warehouses in Kochi's vast harbour, Kerala, India.

WEATHER

The sun isn't always out and shifting weather renders each walk along the same route different. One day wind-devils stir up dust, on another chords of rain obscure the view, hail might pound the leaves off trees, and today does sunlight bounce upon the wet grass beneath your delightful feet?

For each turn, the weather influences somebody - wild waves slapping a beach excite surfers but disappoint swimmers, the southern farmer likes summer rain but holiday makers don't, snow motivates skiers but dismays drivers.

However it presents itself, immerse yourself in the weather, prove you are alive by leaning into the wind, feel the rain scouring your cheeks or the sleet striking your exposed skin. Don't tense up, let the weather untie you. Resisting is escaping, not living in this special moment. Ha! breathe deeply, absorbing this vibrancy.

You'll be in good company. In 1874 the father of the USA's National Parks, John Muir, was in the High Sierra when a fierce storm struck. He rushed up the Yuba River to experience the fury which blew young Sugar Pines flat and rocked "The most steadfast monarchs". Nearing a mountain ridge, he climbed high into a Douglas Spruce and spent hours immersed in the fury with "an invincible gladness"and with his senses in overdrive.

The wind lifts the
book as I draw,
it scoots the dark
clouds over the
moors. My page is
damp soft on
this September

An Atlantic storm rolls across Dartmoor, England.

@
CLOUDS

They sweep past, far, far above our path and we generally ignore them unless a sunset lights them up. Admire these nebulous creations of vapour whipped up and spun about by moving air. Sometimes they are fluffy, other times they seem solid enough to ski down or to even shake a skyscraper.

They can also be the stuff of dreams, removing your mind from worries as the ever shifting shapes and hues transport your imagination. Should you need more than attentive concentration when walking, a simple game can help. Watch the caravan of clouds progress across the sky, weaving a tale which constantly transforms itself. A dog might mutate into a camel which grows a beard and becomes a mad professor striding off on a pilgrimage. You'll be in good company, Constable the English artist said clouds fed his soul.

Clouds enhance the setting sun as a lone fisherman rides incoming waves with his sail down,
Shaviyani Atoll. The Maldives.

You could try predicting the weather awaiting you, mindful of cloud-types before you set off.

Low and heavy strata stuck together (strato-cumulus), pronounce 6 hours of stable 'as-is-now' conditions. Cumulus clouds, the fluffy sheep of the sky, are the sign of fair weather; seen mid morning they mean dry weather till sunset. Beware of isolated giant blobs called cumulo-nimbus which can bring summer storms.

All the more pressing are the small, dark and wispy ghosts hanging beneath other clouds, they tell of imminent rain.

Feathery cirrus clouds announce a depression is 15-24 hours away and if they have thickly set lines, heavy inclemency will come.

A caravan of cumulo-nimbus accompanied our evening walks on a new island in Shaviyani Atoll. The Maldives.

NIGHT

Sometimes, waking in the night I can't get back to sleep. It is perhaps 3am, so I don my clothes and walk quietly around our calm little village, trying not to disturb people with the click-clack of my crutch. I've walked around Delhi, London and other cities, but prefer the countryside in the dark.

Night walks are primal, quite a speciality if you can do so safely. You are aware of being alone, you are conscious of every footstep, every breath. It takes a while to adjust to the dark, things are entirely different, other creatures inhabit the world, gremlins and ghosts are suddenly a possibility.

A clear night sky opens the lid of our little world, presenting us with multiple problems: We are told there are infinite universes out there beyond those sparkling stars; some argue that this universe is alongside other realities, all twisted together like rope; that perhaps a parallel *'us'* is out there.

Picture meeting this being upon a night path - what would you think of 'you'? Try it in a safe place.

With your senses alerted, hover on the edge of your subconscious.

First Snow.

Low night-clouds sweep over a lonely farmstead mid-winter, Derbyshire, England.

MOON

The moon's first thin slither hangs above the crimson sunset and your heart leaps as you step onwards. My mother teased that this was a touch of luck upon your life, but only if not seen through glass; glasses don't count.

Fifteen minutes later, on the following evening, a stronger silver scythe hovers higher above a sunset which has already lost its intensity. How sweet a moment made for romance.

A little later on in the lunar month the moon is fuller and you wonder where time has gone, for the sun has long since fled.

And all too soon a full blown moon lasting deep into the night illuminates the folds of earth, casting shadows below buildings. Magic is in the air. Was that the fox, the owl's shadow, or a phantom?

And now as you wake and do a night walk, our nearest planet is shrinking into another thin curve, now facing the other way. And life is fleeing past but we've hardly noticed.

Such precious moments these, they enrich our hearts - seize them with gusto. Linger with the moon in its various stages, letting its mystery illuminate your emotions.

The same English farm, another season, another angle, and see, the moon shaded hills aren't obscured.

TREES

"Any fool can destroy trees, they can not walk away."

Trees enrich the world. They deposit their leaves, enriching the soil into which they and other trees and fungi reach, sifting it for minerals and water. Each tree is an ecosystem harbouring its own complex micro-environment. Their living foliage senses nibbling insects and they release chemicals to warn one another of attacking swarms.

Trees form a great part of the world's lungs and today we need them more than ever. Because they sup up greenhouse gasses, they can save us.... But our chainsaws are all too quick, which is why women farmers in the Indian Himalaya hugged trees to stop them being felled by illegal loggers.

In southern England some groves of yews are 4,000 years old, they stood when Stonehenge was in active use! We must plant more. In Africa they are planting the fringes of deserts because they understand how vital they are to life.

Trees are the best present you can give.... In our wills, my wife and I will bequeath all our money (this house) to plant hundreds of thousands of these amazing plants. Go on, leave some money to save the world by stocking its forests. Abandon google to search the web using ecosia.com , who plant a tree for every 45 clicks.

Feel an old tree's majesty and strength and time travel in your imagination - did Henry the 8th burp under this oak? Did Descartes *think* he was 'here' beneath this plain tree? Maybe Buddha sat beneath this 3,000 year old deodar?

"(Trees) grip the ground as though they like it...."

Both quotes - John Muir, inspiration for America's National Parks.

Unconcerned by the busy traffic, spirits eternally inhabit discarded spirit houses placed beneath this holy bodi tree.

tree too complicated to hug, with 'spirit houses'. Chiang Mai, Thailand.

EARTH

Soil so humble, so essential, bursts with billions of beings which thrive by interacting. Our soil, enriched by dead plants and animals being recycled. This earth, this ordinary material, the stuff we take for granted, ultimately produces everything we eat, for it gives all creatures the nutrients required to live. Our oceans are dusted with its minerals, enabling plankton, the base of the marine food chain, to thrive.

With your foot, test the ground, is it moist? dry or frosty? Dig your fingers in and feel the texture, is it crumbly, grainy or clayish? Roll it in your palm, smell it, relish it. Imagine what it might taste like. Linger, linger.

I once met a lorry driver who, as he drove, composed poetry about the soils he passed over. For two million years we have increasingly controlled nature. Today, even in the wildest corners of the Himalayas, deposits are found from the many chemicals we use daily. One day the soil will absorb residue from the shampoos, soaps and pollutants released from our decaying bodies. Even in nature respecting Britain, farmers churn up and impact the soil using heavy machinery, threatening to deaden its fertility by the year 2050. We are deeply in debt and utterly linked to the soil. Perhaps as you walk you'd like to make a vow to protect it as best you can.

We are connected to the Earth. It depends on our spending habits. We are responsible for the demands we put on farmers for cheaper food. Think of future generations and the world's dwindling list of creatures, by buying local, sustainable food which has not laced the ground with harmful chemicals; though slightly more costly, is well worth it. And, do you really need that new item of clothing?

*Remains of a burnt old shepherd's hut turning back into soil,
Spanish Pyrenees.*

SETTLING

*The first **flash-awareness** session. Engrain it at home. Each of these should eventually last 1-2 minutes, however, until established they will take longer.*

The breathing part is often used by emergency workers to calm themselves when in danger; soldiers crossing cold winter rivers are taught deep breathing prevents them panicking and helps their bodies to adjust.

Settling.
Step off the path, pause and note the soil beneath your feet. Appreciate the foliage, the colours, the light, the air and the weather where you are.

Be aware of your shifting chest as your gliding breath shifts your shoulders, pulses your neck, leaves your throat, quits your nostrils.

Take a slow deep breath; hold it for 6 heart beats. Enjoy the subtle pause. Slowly, very very slowly, let it go.
Repeat this cycle 6 times (no more!).

Loiter with interest where your spine meets the reptilian brain and relish a flash-awareness of you, sensual, whole.
A being created over billions of years, someone to be respected, cherished, adored*.

How magnificent! Chuckle, do a wiggle-dance like a comedian having a ball. (or not?)

Now hum, "How lucky I am!" (silently?)

*Repetition of '**Settling**' engrains and magnifies it. Master 'Settling' and enjoy it anywhere, for it will become your secret cove.*

*Whether stressed or calm, habitually **uniting** each section's **micro-boosts** as one exercise will intensify your walking experience. Regularly stop walking for a few seconds, lingering with each **boost** as it sinks in. Before reaching home, no matter which of this book's sections you have got to, stop and enjoy this '**Settling**' flash-awarenesses for two minutes.*

MRI video-scans show the simple act of appreciating something triggers those parts of the brain which act together to lift our mood. Appreciating the self, what could be better?

Survivors of tsunamis, war devastation or earthquakes, people who've lost family, home, community, *everything*, gradually gain equanimity with micro-boosts. They are taught to habitually hone-in on detail - light on a flower, the feel of a stone, anything, without adding value, rapidly looking, sensing, moving on.

Such repetitive stimulation of the brain enhances neural connectivity… energised, stimulated, we feel alive.

Imagine
the effect of constantly appreciating
what you are,
where you are.
Imagine
if we all did.
Imagine
such a world.

* *This is genuine deep admiration for the biological wonder 'self', not shallow ego-driven self worship.*

FOOT

Nature gave us the wheel and you can discover this by making a video of yourself taking a few steps with a red dot stuck to your ankle. You will see that this spot forms a circle as the ankle elevates, the toes raise, the foot lifts, moves forwards and the heel is finally set back down. If you don't drag your feet, this circular motion improves efficiency and lessens effort - it is partly why we walk more efficiently than flat-footed apes who scuffle along.

Perhaps using the excuse of peering at a bird in a bush, observe every movement from your heel to toe by stepping very, very slowly. As you do, sink your attention into your foot as it pivots forward, minutely noticing this sophisticated human marvel. Clever old evolution created a marvel we take for granted.

Then there's the ankle's stunning joint which swivels 360 degrees yet is still able to prevent us falling on tricky ground, to say nothing of the toes which help us balance.

Any one of these high-tech features is a feat of engineering robots still fail to emulate, but making them work together is verging on the magical. Lucky you!

Upon a clean beach or on unpolluted grass, take off your shoes and with great attention rediscover why infants prefer to walk barefoot!

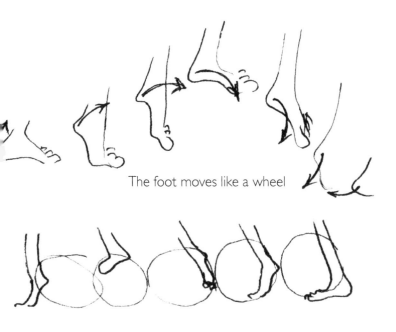

The foot moves like a wheel

We were designed to walk barefoot. Athletes wearing Olympic standard shoes strike the ground with their heel, whereas barefoot Kenyan runners land on the ball of their feet; impact is far less so they don't suffer the back and joint aches which plague athletes.

b
SHADE-TEXTURE

Early in the morning or on a grey day the sky is flat, the light levelled. As your circular foot motion rolls you forwards, cast your eye around. **Pick out the subtle shade created by foliage or buildings which cut down the light-load falling upon the ground. Don't hurry, be scientific. Look at your hand under unadulterated light and again when inside a doorway or beneath a large tree. Shift it about, noticing how less brightness illuminates your skin. Examine how light's intensity shifts all over your walking body.** Linger, child-like. It's quite magical, these micro-boosts are designed to still you.

Since we stopped working the land where we were showered by 20,000 lux* on a grey winter's day, our species has spent most of its day indoors where 200 lux is average. This lack-lustre light invades our moods, for the animal organ which is the brain assumes it is time to wind down and prepare for sleep, so you are not depressed, simply a little glum. Don't despair, going for a walk early in the morning helps, as does making excuses to stand by a large window as often as possible. But nothing beats being bathed in summer's 100,000 lux.

When the light is uniform it is interesting to compare the texture of things, that leaf, those bricks, the path you are walking along, your very skin with days when the sun is out. However, diffused light creates an allure photographers love. **Attune yourself to these differences, radiate your days by becoming a connoisseur of luminescence.**

* Mid-latitude USA, China or Europe.

The sun's luminosity bouncing off the water, infecting the holiday makers, igniting the trees, adding to the magic in Salcombe, Devon, England.

ⓑ
EMOTION

A friend's walks are often driven by raving emotion. Emotion is part of our chemical feedback system in which neuro-chemicals regulate our organism, sending messages to cells which help us survive.

When walking you can stroll through emotion, aware of what is happening inside you. **Watch these whirlpools without engagement and as your fascination increases, you'll recognise aspects of your persona. Learn to contend with them.** Emotion is grouped into:- PROTECTIVE - Fear *(anxiety)*; Rage *(self protection)*; Panic *(abandonment, loss, sadness, loneliness)*. NURTURING - Lust *(creative urge)*, Caring *(love, compassion)*; Play *(learning, joyousness)*; Seeking *(exploring, enthusiasm)*.

Bend down and stroke a passing cat or dog, for compassion (ie caring) is built by contact; mothers naturally stroke their babies, animals respond to being stroked. There's strange things going on too. When feeling love, interferon, a chemical which fights viruses, is produced inside us to ensure we're fit enough to look after any subsequent offspring. **Step out rippling with those positive emotions - playfulness, caring, creativity, and 'seeking' - as you watch your inner whirlwinds!**

Changing from a negative mental habit is hard, for without our realising it, our under-mind finds negative emotion fascinating. It is filled with dangers we need to survey. **But remember that practice makes perfect and turn your walks into zippy therapy sessions** and after about 66 days, a flick of thought ought to rise you above the quagmire (which continues). Knowing 'You' in all your mess and glory enables you to like yourself for being a normal human. This is how we are!

Emotion rippled through me and the sacredness of this ancient site was forgotten when a stone thrown by a wayward lad struck the page as I drew Shiva's timeless temples. Jageshwar, Kumaon Himalaya, India.

VEXED BEARS

As you move one foot in front of the other, are you swirling on about something your parent said years ago? Perhaps you're blasting yourself for not being a great success, maybe you're irritated by some aspect of your behaviour? Join the club! We're full of vexed bears. It's often due to the way we've been brought up. Volleys of "No!", "Do this!" or "You must....!" can constantly undermine children, they can feel they can't do right, if so, self-criticism and insecurity become built-in.

Some parents create an atmosphere within which rules aren't dictated but arise from consensual discussion about the way forwards. Phrases such as: "Oops, is that wise?" "What happens if you do this?" "Touch with your eyes," grant a child the authority to think for itself and alter its behaviour. If done unskilfully though, the child can develop into a self-will, self-centred egoist. Not good. When a child is in a strop, if the mother calmly asks, "Can you find words for how you feel?" it helps the child develop emotional intelligence. Not only does the youngster feel secure, but they learn self-awareness and how to explore inner issues verbally.

Facing our inner bears, we can also discover these strong emotional whirlpools are not necessarily ours, but were imposed upon us by society's bluster. As you step off, **grasp the ideas behind your vexations, untangle them and release the negative emotions they create.** Bear-fully delighted to have broken free from convention and to be thinking for yourself, Baloo-dance ever onwards.

Drawing these barns at -12 C made me face my inner bears.
Near Dortmund, Germany.

DISCRIMINATE

As you walk you might be toying with a dozen or more thought clusters - this evening's meal, a relationship, a vital project, some future adventure. The mind decides which to pay attention to, which to log, which to act on. Sloppy mental discipline means many of us are irritated that we twirl from one such cluster to another willy-nilly. Some subsequently try to stop thought's antics, hoping to rise to a super-human buddha-realm. Impossible! Thought is a natural brain activity, not an enemy. Even Buddha thought - ample proof lies in his logical discourses. Thought helps us explore all sides of a situation and find solutions. But how to control the ranting monkey? The cool mindset we are gradually building herein helps us select thought-patterns with greater skill.

When a top London barrister constantly dealing with life's ugly side became devastatingly depressed, a renowned psychiatrist advised walking *attentively* as the best therapy. Whilst walking we have purpose - to move forwards and this helps to dislocate our attention from what's going on inside. Continually illuminating our minds with observations (p34) adds power to the process, enabling us to eventually perceive our lives from a better perspective.

Also acknowledge your thoughts as your feet roll along, but concentrate on the minute oscillations of your body and mull over the multi-sensual experience of moving through this fascinating world.

Light-hearted purpose is the key.

Discriminating, but suppressing criticism, I drew the pundit outlining everyone's horoscopes as a lad with a catapult scared birds off the fruit trees. Kumaon Himalaya, India.

ⓑ

MINDSETS

We glide along life's pathways not really aware of why we think as we do. Today as you walk, glance at yourself with a smile*. It is helpful to think in terms of 'mindsets', consolidated attitudes which prop us up, make us who we are, define our world, ignite our sense of purpose.

By our 7th year, as we struggled to survive our early experiences, our base-mindsets are embedded. Those mindsets we inhabited most dominated, became traits, fixed our character. Yet nothing is permanent for the brain is plastic and if we *really* want to, with effort we can change. First we must understand our outlook, see how it directs our days and decide upon the mental slant with which we wish to proceed.

Should you doubt our psychological flexibility, consider that a person who generally sees life as dull falls in love and suddenly everything is bright. However, when they discover their beloved is secretly having as much fun with another, their new outlook, built on hope rather than on a substantial fresh world view, crumbles and their shallow 'vision' transmutes into rage, which colours everything.

If, despite today's beautiful walk, you catch yourself stuck in a state you wish to change but assume you can't, think of the unjustly imprisoned who survive mentally intact; it has been found they lift themselves above despair at the utter misery. If they can, so can we. **Embrace your various attitudes and traits, allow this new awareness to** slowly **evolve into a new mindset and stride onwards.**

* Unbelievably, smiling generates endorphins! Watch the video-link - P16

46

Aït Souka

Grumbling in the intense heat made me stop under a walnut tree and change mindsets by drawing this suspended village in the dry High Atlas, Morocco.

WEBS

On misty mornings spiders' webs quiver in the breeze. Don't hurry past but hesitate and take in the diffused light sparkling off a thousand dewdrops. Circles of diamonds strung one within the other! At the edge of each web anchor ropes stronger than steel stretch out to grip surrounding foliage, each glistens with water beads. **Feel amazed, allow enthusiasm to well within**.

Further across the park or field, in the hedges there's the even finer strings making up orb webs. These tubes of mesh curl expertly in a cone that entraps insects seeking dark corners away from the dangers of the wide open world. Lucky insects on sparkling misty mornings.

Go on a web hunt and thrill yourself by taking snaps from many angles if you haven't the time or inclination to draw them. Did you see any of the expert engineers who created these incredible structures? Marvel at the minute majesty before you. Nature's magic can untangle us from the inner webs we might be stuck within.

What emotional or thought webs entrap you upon today's wheel-walk?* Circles of angst about something unresolved? Anger at the way you are treated by certain individuals? Ho ho, so typically human!

SMILE
at yourself.

* Remember your foot's circular motion, P36.

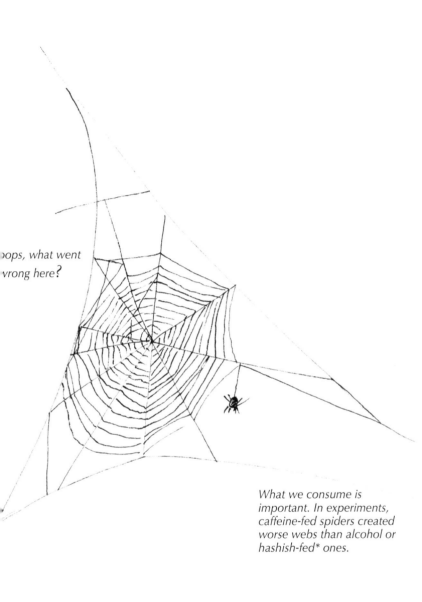

oops, what went wrong here?

What we consume is important. In experiments, caffeine-fed spiders created worse webs than alcohol or hashish-fed* ones.

* !Not recommended!!

She's decorating my shed.

INSECTS

They sweep about us and we all but ignore them as we plough onwards, unless a genuine allergy fill us with fear or an irritating mosquito lands on our skin. Yet insects were here long before humanity evolved and they will continue long after our self-imposed demise. Speaking of which, cockroaches and ants will adapt to Climate Change better than we, so respect these generally innocuous creatures.

Take flies. Flies, a marvel of creation, have the most boggling eyes. And being nature's jump-jet, they can take off at any angle. Talking of jumping, the flea jumps faster than an accelerating racing car. And bees were once wasps which became vegetarians, a smart move which adapted to the arrival of flowers and even influenced the growth and variety of flora. Talk about longevity, short-lived dragonflies existed before the dinosaurs stomped this land we now walk over. We, because of our madnesses, could soon be as extinct as the many creatures we've already spun into oblivion.

One spring afternoon millions of migrating bugs brought the Himalayan settlement of Dharmsala to a halt. Tibetan refugees rushed from their homes and shops, emerged from their vehicles, blocking the streets. Careful not to step on any living thing, people gently lifted the insects to the nearest bushes.

Upon your journeys help nature just a little by bending down and, with a stiff leaf, lift a beetle or a snail out of harm's way. On a cold or dank summer's day, let a tired bee sip a drop of honey. A simple act of compassion, a simple thing to help the little creatures which are keystone to our many ecosystems and our very future.

PATHS

Your walk can be augmented by observing the flurry of creatures scurrying about. **Hesitate, peep in to the bushes, note that all around us there are paths made by creatures big and tiny.** They weave their tracks in every direction, ignoring or crossing our own routes, hopeful they will get to where they want without being squashed by foot or tyre.

Look closer, the undergrowth is littered with them, the soil shows their passage, soft surfaces are patterned with little footprints weaving here and there. We are not always able to tread lightly, often in a hurry, we innocently trample these ignored highways, ending the lives of parents seeking food for their young. If attentive upon our habitual paths, we get to know where these minute routes are and we can exercise caution as we approach them.

Enrich your walks by discovering a new layer of transport weaving through the landscape. Admire, rather than accidentally stamping on insect routes when next you tread your favourite path. In such ways, our walks become our guides, leading us towards a greater understanding of nature's interwoven systems. A recent study underscored the positive effect of observing nature - little tendrils of brightness and compassion seep into our daily existence.

HISTORY

All that has happened before influences the NOW and walking with an awareness of history intensifies our present. The paths our ancestors carved upon the earth's surface wind through vegetation, tracing the easiest way forwards. In certain places in England deep ravines called holloways (*hola weg* in Saxon) were created by 3-5 thousand years of walking livestock to fields or markets, loosening the surface, enabling flooding rain to gradually dig groves which can be over ten metres deep.

Wherever we are, our forebears seem lost in time, but they have handed down hedgerows, smoothed off ancient ditches, mounds, canals, walls. **Seek them out and with each step over stone or groove laid in the past, contemplate what those distant people might have felt and seen. Reach down, touch the landscape they imprinted.**

We who pass in the flick of a moment and whose lives are almost as fleeting, ought to admire our patrimony and comprehend our vital role in preserving that which has been handed down to us.

Furthermore, what we do now will be here for our offspring's offspring to see and criticise. Ensure you tread lightly upon our precious Earth!

The roots of an ancient ash work their way into sandstone laid down 100,000,000 years ago. The forces of nature will be here long after this old retaining wall and the house it protects in the French Pyrenees have crumbled.

THE EDGE

You arrive at a drop and stand a little way back, concerned you could fall. You shiver as your mind considers leaping into the void. You step further away, convinced a self-destructive urge impels you. This mad impulse last happened in a shop amidst rows of delicate cut-glass which you wanted to shatter. Another time you wanted to strike out at your boss.

You shudder. Sure there's something wrong with you. Somewhere deep inside you must be maniacal, aggressive, suicidal even.

There's nothing wrong!

It happens to all creatures.

And for a reason.

It is how the brain works.

We imagine scenarios to prepare ourselves for danger or to ensure social norms are not breached. You can sigh with relief, you'll not leap off that cliff, lose your job or be imprisoned for running amok in that shop! A coiled rope awakening the fear of snakes is better than being bitten by the real thing.

However, we humans have a tendency to make the world fit our preconceptions, for the brain believes what we tell it. Our culture's tales may make us believe there's ghosts in the graveyard or gods in the sky. This helped us group together with common purpose. And attack those who thought differently. Our ability to visualise has given us the arts, which expanded our lateral thinking, without which we'd still be stuck in freezing caves concerned about snakes. It enabled us to contemplate our general situation, to picture walls and doors, create ethical rules, write books and make movies.

Next time fear makes you step back, appreciate your positively prudent mind working for your own good.

Upon the edge of white cliffs, East Devon, England.

EDDIES

They feed our bodies and imaginations, no wonder we call them freshets, becks, burns, bourns, brooks, rivulets, runnels, streamlets, watercourses.

In 'Siddhartha', Hermann Hesse's main character gained wisdom from watching the flow of a river. Doing so relaxes the mind, takes us a few strokes from our tense inner currents. Recent research has found that being beside the sea, a lake, pond or river boosts our mood. It might be the extra light being reflected back at us*....

We rise into lighter eddies where objectivity is prevalent and, seen from above, the depths of our egocentric muck and mire seem trivial. We identify with the wider picture obscured from far below, seeing fountains of possibility and streams of freedom flowing from our swamp.

Like our minds, a watercourse contains many little environments entwined together. There are creatures and plants which thrive in sandy shallows, those which prefer fast flowing water and others found only in deep pools, to say nought of the myriad holes in the banks which hold the flow. These walls retaining the river, worn smooth by centuries of flooding, contain shapes which hold the mind, each curve, texture and colour tinted by the light bouncing off the water's surface.

Allow a rill or a river to gush you from your habitual thoughts so that you can enjoy a life more open. Cascade, surge and spate with glee as you slip onwards!

*Remember P38?

The very start of the river Aspe, French Pyrenees.

REFLECTION

Water, without it we soon die, yet too much and it is dangerous. Water magnifies our immersed hand and distorts it, making it appear bent. That pebble we try to grab seems to move. The surface shimmers and changes with the wind or due to hidden forces within. The sky is held at our feet, as are the curving hills. This elusiveness encourages wariness, fear mingles with awe.

Standing beside a puddle or a lake, **have fun swaying from side to side, shaking reflected buildings, hills and stout trees. Laugh - how mighty you are! Allow the flicker of reflected colours and shapes to draw you in. Slip back in time, ponder how our ancestors would have viewed water. Is that somebody else peering back? This stuff is magic! It must be a portal into other worlds.**

Water reflects sunlight, just the Lux restorative we need! It is mysterious, things we don't understand must exist. A screech-owl's bloody cry speeds over a pool in the dead of night, our spines chill, our imagination goes into overdrive and embedded tales from childhood pop open. Mysterious forces must direct our lives; help, ghouls! We trust in 'fate'.

Our ancestors believed spring water heals. Others living beside streams over the mountain thought differently, and because we didn't invent their ideas, we disliked them. We fought, we killed, and all over a shimmering mirage. However, inside, we still have a childish mindset as yet unpolluted by stiff cultural judgement. **Standing over a puddle, open it up and let its innocence soften your adult assumptions. Sink into contemplation, feel yourself stilling.**

IMMERSION

The sensual input your brain prioritises is *vision*.

Stop mid walk and take in your surroundings,
abstractly enjoying the world before you.

Analyse your surroundings, note the many shades
and textures as if you were about to paint a
monochrome picture such as those in this book.

Observe and admire signs of insect or animal life.

Feel the emotion the scene creates within you.

Note your dominating mindset, discriminate;
shift from it if needed.

Mentally reside at the top of your spine,
where sensory input arrives in the brain.
Feel yourself in the safest place imaginable.
Know you are animal, ape, human,
utterly you,
strong, poised, alive!

Appreciate this magical moment which your
bewildering history has lead you to.

Smile,
chuckle (quietly?) with delight.

A crumbling wall, The Lake District, England.

ℂ
ERECT

Ever wondered why walking upright was such a doddle? OK, we have the help of twelve leg muscles, but so do apes who waddle upright for short distances in an ungainly fashion which strains their bodies, and is both incompetent and exhausting. No wonder they prefer knuckle crawl-walking. **Try that for a laugh, but out of sight!** (and on a soft surface)

In contrast, our elegant efficiency is good for the body because our joint friction and torque are low. This enables us to enjoy walking miles and miles on any terrain, if we are up to it.

Poor apes, their shorter legs drop straight from the outside of a wide pelvis, placing their feet far apart, they also have weak pelvic muscles, as a consequence, their bodies swing from side to side with each step. **Be ape once again and try walking with your heels shoulder width apart and knees well bent. And laugh. In comparison, how developed our stride!**

Human thigh bones angle in from our smaller pelvis to the knee, placing our feet centrally and our pelvic muscles are strong. These points ensure a stable, upright posture and an easy gait.

Walking upright is a great advantage, our eyes don't stick to the ground or into the bushes so we can see further, which is safer. Our hands are free to fashion a stone tool, grip the map, hold another's fingers and still we can touch that flower.

Did evolution recall the antelope's and horse's front legs and mould those on to our wondrous feet?
A surefooted pack horse. Kumaon Himalaya, India.

ℂ

STANCE

Although built to be erect, we learn to stand and walk to suit the manner our society prefers. Across rural Africa and India people stand and walk tall. We admire their elegance, wish we were like them, but should we do this in our own society, we can be seen as assertive, verging on the arrogant or aggressive*. We subsequently learn to slouch, then suffer with tense muscles in the lower back, shoulder, bottom and upper legs**.

The pelvis is our keystone. Its orientation determines how the spine rests and moves, and strong abdominal muscles hold us upright, easing the strain on our back and shoulder muscles.

Try walking imagining you are suspended by a string rising from your crown. You'll find you are more upright.

* At college in England, I was told my African stance looked arrogant, I tried to adopt the slouch, but soon gave up.
** The plank exercise strengthens these, but start gently.

A farmer upright on his way to market, Kumoan Himalaya, India. (That was his horse loaded with apples on P65)

C

FEELING

At 3 square metres and weighing almost three kilos, your skin is your largest organ. And armed with keratin, melanin and oils, it comes in three layers. Our bespoke raincoat the epidermis, also protects us from invading germs. Our dermis, the middle coat, not only flexes and strengthens, but senses pressure, pain and temperature. Our innermost suit, the hypodermis, insulates us.

The tips of your fingers have webs of nerves which enable you to define your world more sensitively than even your ancestors the chimps. You can turn the pages of this book, probably reproduce these drawings and do a host of other dextrous non-chimp things. **Rub your thumb and fingers together to test the air** - crisp to your skin on a dry day, slightly sticky on a damp one, syrupy upon a summer's beach.

Reach out and sense the undulations of that broad leaf. Is it ribbed, somewhat smooth, pliable? Beware though, some are prickly. Lean in and if nobody is watching or if you care not, let your cheek gently rub its surface, allowing your skin to sense it minutely. Immerse yourself in child-like wonder, nothing exists but this, hold the moment. Lips, more sensitive, will increase the sensual input… if you dare! When in stressful situations, feeling your finger tips distracts, calms. It is potent!

Relish being sufficiently alive to do this crazy thing. Time is fleeting and a day will come when you'll desperately wish you could. When we touch another our skins resonate, we each pick up information; curiously, when we touch our own heart-areas, our brains assume somebody kind is touching us with care. In various cultures, this gesture is taken as a sign of heart-felt sincerity.

*Waxy plants outside my window in a village
near the Thai-Burmese border.*

C

SOUND

Air rushes over the ridge, howls between the buildings, plucks the grass, twangs the branches, rattles leaves and debris. **Feel it upon your skin, sense it in your ears, see how it affects your stance, your mood, even your eyes.** Dogs and children react, becoming more excited, which dog-walkers enjoy but teachers dislike.

These noises form waves which enter your ear, vibrate the drum, causing three tiny bones to hammer a tissue, which in turn quivers a fluid-filled shell containing hair cells. These tremble, pulsating electrical signals which nerves carry to the brain. Beat that for innovation!

Sound transports your mind. Watch a horror film without the soundtrack and it is not as powerful, **so let your ears catch the squeal from strained telephone lines, the sea-like roar of blustered woods, a wind-sprite screeching through a tunnel. Get up early one morning and tune in to a blackbird playing with the thrush's composition or transmute the pigeon's coos into a micro-meditation*.**

As you walk, feel your ears picking up the sounds around you, this 'sensing' is more than listening. Sound enchants the present - it is partly why we love listening to music. Snow deadens sound, hushing busy roads, adding to winter's magic. Bees and the sound of summer pastures soothe the 'heart' and recalling them can help us find sleep, as can listening to your body's noises.

* ie, a micro-boost.

Screaming stone walls inspired me to stop, listen and sketch upon a long winter trek across Snowdonia, North Wales, Britain.

ℂ
DISTANCE

The eye-lens bulges when looking at something close and flattens to gaze at distant objects. Two eyes enable creatures to perceive distance by combining signals from slightly different angles. At the same time, the brain compares the size of similar objects near and far, also analysing their perceived texture and detail before computing how far away something is. Astonishing!

Stand and let your eyes fall comfortably on an object two metres distant. Hold your breath whilst appreciating this fence, door nob, flower or lamp post. Slowly, meaningfully, release the air in your lungs, allowing your vision to travel to something double the distance, 'feel' the increased gap as your vision lands on this object. Breathe in, hold it, acutely observing the new item and the increased volume before you.

Repeat these steps according to the time you have available. Your gaze may end up just across the way or far off. **At each point, sense the space expanding before you.** Exercising your perception in this manner sets you in place and is another way to enhance your walks.

*Gazing over summer barns, now holiday homes, along an old
drove track reaching far above Aulon,
Saint Lary, French Pyrenees.*

HORIZONS

Your bouncy feet take you to the summit and the world drops away. **Stand erect and appreciate the view for a while, trying not to analyse, dissect or label what you see. There, upon this elevated spot, simply enjoy and smile - how fortunate you are!**

Allow your eye to flow with the textures of light, with the shapes defining the landscape, be it city or country, seascape or desert. See those terraced houses or is it hedges or sand ridges stitching it all together?

Enjoy the movement, be it birds scooting far away or cars upon that city route so small from up here. For a short while, be the demigod of all you survey.

This moment will never be repeated
and it is yours.
**Take charge of it,
twirl it about in your metaphorical hands.**

Can you sense something unusual? Something a little strange? Has your mind stilled, opening you to a sensation of other-worldliness? It is nothing odd, esoteric or religious.

You are in awe of the ever-unfolding present.
It is a mental space our tribal cousins know well*.
Or what the cat feels as it purrs upon your lap.
A natural moment.
I lap it up.

* I can vouch for this, as I grew up in the Kenyan bush.

I was soon to be covered in white by those summer snow-laden clouds obscuring the Italian horizon above Modane, The French Alps.

ℂ

UPLIFT

There are days when you step in to a room (at work?) or eyes which turn to engage and your brain slides backwards, seeking the pillow.

At such times, be you in your bathroom facing your own reflected eyes or out in the cruel world, **gently (unobtrusively?), shake yourself alive, paying attention to the ripple of flesh in each limb.**

Take a deep breath and stand tall**, legs apart. Absolutely** tall**, body lightly suspended by a silk thread attached to the top of your crown.** This also works when leaning back in a chair with your hands folded behind your neck, elbows extended sideways.

Holding these erect postures for two minutes does something interesting. The brain assumes we are defending ourselves against a mighty ape and pumps 15% more testosterone into our many systems, preparing us to snarl or scamper (with a first class ticket).

This involuntary reaction happens in both sexes, and don't worry, a little of the big 'T' helps. We feel ready to face those eyes, able to stride out and be 'Me'. But don't over-play the 'trump' card, you may regret it.

Standing tall after all these years, South Bishop Lighthouse before a storm, Pembrokeshire, Wales.

PERSONALITY

What sort of personality do you have? Have you changed over the years? I was once an open extrovert, an agreeable 'life and soul of the party'. I am still unabashed, but poor health has dampened me, now I'm hardly noticeable....

We humans are a complex mix of many character influences and these have been simplified into 5 interconnected Meta Traits -

Open (creative), Extrovert (social), Conscientious (planner), Agreeable (kind), Neurotic (insecure).

Watch yourself with a tinge of amusement and discover who you are. Are you driven to achieve predetermined results, are you more concerned with comfort, are relationships your priority?

You could, for example, be 20% creative, 15% social, 20% planner, 20% kind, 25% insecure, or are you completely different?

This is a useful exercise if we are candid, it helps us balance ourselves, our lives and our relationships, if we adjust the traits we discover within.

Le Chateau Chinon
La Loire, France

ℂ
PREJUDICE

Do you see yourself as a lone wolf, part of a group or a mix of these? Are you mentally part of a subculture, a citizen of a specific place, a member of a continent or do you see yourself as one being amongst all the others cluttering up our tiny planet?

Whole cultures are gripped by particular mindsets. Take Sub Himalayan Asia where various cultures lived alongside one another until 1948 when the British divided them into three countries. This created endless tension which continues today. Mega-mindsets infect humanity as a whole. For example, for decades swathes of the world have increasingly been gripped by abject self-indulgence, which fuels consumerism.

Notice what these mega-mindsets tell you about yourself. Are you open to the influences each culture has upon yours? Do you disregard or degrade those from other subsets or societies? In other words, are you rigid or more plastic? Can you discover why you are like this?

Would you like to adjust this vantage? People say they can't, but the mind is elastic hence malleable, but if we are stuck in our preoccupations and assumptions we aren't willing to change. **Be alert, be positive, try acting and change these interlinked traits, you'll be liberating the claws of the past.**

The much admired new mosque,
Mattancherry, Fort Kochi, Kerala, India.

ℂ
BIAS

As we stroll along, what we see is tinged by what we think, which is what our micro-culture's mindsets trained us to think. We might see a romantic grove of trees where that person sees wood to harvest sustainably and the next finds a beauty spot within which he could build a house. We might take those others who think differently as dreamers, country-bumpkins or environmental rapists. Each one of us is convinced we are right because of the bias we cling to. Yet that copse isn't as we perceive it to be, its character is formed by a collection of interacting plants and creatures struggling to survive.

We might see that thicket as a haven for nature, if saved it will benefit us and our off-spring, for nature's abundance provides for everyone in the long run. Our brain incessantly seeks our best interests, trading present rewards against future gains. Mental agility is not only a refined skill, it is extremely helpful. Shifting and weighing up contrasting vantages in a situation helps us see clearly and discover our specific way forwards.

Passing that spinney, stop, stand tall, absorb the sounds emanating from the trees and bushes, feel the cool they provide on a hot day, the shelter on a stormy one.

Take a deep breath, mindfully let it out a few times and when your mind is a little clearer, see the branches and leaves as they are. Try to see your current mindset and bias towards this place. Note the words you used to depict this copse. Words are powerful coagulations of thought, so assist yourself by having an arsenal of contrasting words to fire at your bias and to help you shift aside from it - a great technique used to move bad habits.

She sees dinner, the fishermen see sport, French speaking tourists chuckled at a romantic French moment. Drawing, absorbed by these medieval houses, even though I heard her, I missed her for when I looked up she had gone....
L'Aude River, Limoux, France.

HABITS

Caught in some habit or other as you move along a stretch of track? Habits are formed because the brain condenses registered lines of repetitive action into shortcuts to save energy. MRI scans show these are tight electrical nodules, rather than the extended strings casual actions and thoughts create. Habits accumulate thoughts, forming ever stronger mindsets and we admire these, assuming they make up 'Me'. This is partially true, but we are also the complex result of evolution, culture, clan, family and personal history, what we've done, what we want and partly what we've eaten.

Habits can blight our lives with negative or unproductive mindsets which create dullness; if we wish to shift from these ruts it requires commitment. **Catching a habit you'd like to change, sympathise and understand this aspect of yourself. Slowly, intensely, begin the preferred thought or action, continually reminding yourself it takes two weeks to establish, a month to consolidate, 2 to 8 months to utterly change. Assist your mind by having an arsenal of good words and moods to continually fire at those habits you want rid of.**

One way is simple - diverting attention to find pleasure in small things. **When washing, let the soap bubbles be magical orbs; allow the light in somebody's eyes to be a spark of their spirit.** Each such engagement removes you from the habit, making this moment relevant, not your disfavoured mindset. Gradually, bit by bit, **you discover happiness within each second as you enjoy what is around you,** be it when walking, breathing or eating. This becomes a habit, eventually a new persona emerges who finds loads of pleasurable in-the-moment experiences! **Go on, engrain the present!**

Habitually, drawing takes me in to a calm mindset.
Europa mountains, Spain.

✳
GAMES & MOODS

We convince ourselves we are this or that, or that we are a mess. Yet few of us have evolved out of emotions and mindsets solidified by our 7th birthday.... It explains a lot.   Here's a way out of our infantile human trap.

Stand tall, *flash-admiring* your physical being.
As you breathe deeply, abstractly notice your senses at play.
Take a deep breath, hold in the tension of physical, emotional and mental activity, relishing these intertwined forces.

Let out the air and **Chuckle!**
How amusingly theatrical our habits, biases and personalities are! Adore yourself for being human.

Breathe in, accepting that this is how we are.
Whoosh out the air you've been holding.
Look into the distance, create your own inner horizon.
Smile!

Give yourself a hug (secretly?), go on! You deserve it.
Linger here for a while.

This vital egoless self-kindness will enable you to sink into the calm mindset you've been developing, and this will help your 'being' thrive, rather than your habitual ego.

Watch the smile video indicated on P168.

An old wooden windmill above a flour mill,
near Linkoping, Sweden.

d

BALANCE

Balance is key to everything we do. Loss of balance increases awkwardness, both physical and mental, injury too. Balancing increases bone and muscle strength, core strength, firmness of the ankles, hips, glutens and most importantly, our spines. Our reflexes, joint dynamics and posture improve. The brain stimulates the mind, amazingly, anxiety decreases, mental clarity increases. It's why athletes do specific balance training.

The brain's reptilian nodule instructs the body to continually rebalance. **Marvel at the mechanism which evolved inside every creature in our lineage.** Our inner ear evolved three differently oriented semi circular tubes filled with liquid which send balancing messages to the brain. **Step along a plank laid on the ground, dead easy. Close your eyes, it's harder** because visual information helps the brain double check gravity's pull. That's why crossing that plank when it is suspended upon a wall two metres high is testing.

Stop walking, stand on each foot. Eyes closed now, balance again. Wobbling? Eyes open, raise one foot and hold this posture alternatively on each foot for 10-15 seconds, gradually increasing to 1 minute. Concentrating helps. When adept, stand on both tip-toes, hold it 10-15 seconds. Walk on your toes from time to time as if creeping up on somebody. Notice your back, bottom, leg, ankle and feet muscles playing to hold you upright. What a wonder. Do a little skip!

* Balance is so important, I've included 3 web-links on P168.

One day as we were walking
through the jungle a
man we knew ran
up a tall tree and
fetched us two young nuts to drink.

Only try this once your balancing skills (and insurance!)
are secure and, aged 104, you want a quick way out....
Farukolhu-Funadhoo, Shaviyani Atoll, The Maldives.

TONGUE TIED

You've probably told a close friend about your favourite walk without considering that language implement in your mouth. The tongue is a Multi-Tool - it talks, it moves food around the mouth, it tastes and helps with smelling. If protruded, it can be provocative, not that it'd be wise to pull a Maori face at another walker. If it were a product it would sell out in minutes. But don't be tempted to lick a frozen tap as you walk past, you'll stick there until somebody rescues you.

Snorting the air as it flits past, you're using your tongue to help detect odour - a subtle flower, a musty animal, though avoid oral gymnastics near pig farms or beside busy highways. If you are walking a dog, appreciate that its sense of smell is 400 times greater than yours, because our human ancestors put more energy into developing sight and sound. Yet there are individuals whose smell is strongly developed; by sniff-tasting the air, Kenyan tribesmen can tell if antelope are near. Being attentive to the aromas entering our noses, we can create a keener awareness - French schools train children to smell and taste - food, of course!

Pretend you are an alien not long arrived from an internal planet, (your mother's womb) who is excited by the novelty of planet Earth's pleasures. Inhale, aware of the minutest hints of perfume or mustiness alerting the olfactory cells in your nostrils and tongue, (hopefully far from rotting litter).

Allow yourself to **dawdle and be dazed, tasting** spring's freshness upon chewed beech leaves! the earthy smell of damp soil… the comfort of mown grass; ah, a rose! the bark of a tree! the purity of sea air.

The smell of hay and wild herbs, Kinnekulle, Sweden.

d

TRUST

Trust your self, for if your mind isn't in conflict with your brain, your body knows what to do. When stepping across a steep rocky stretch, if the souls of your feet are secure, the rest of you ought to be in balance.

This spreads into an innate physical-belief. Having grown up in the unpredictable African bush, I have trusted myself, even in dangerous situations. Until now, this has been rewarded - when moving along thin, icy mountain ridges; when near wild animals; perhaps foolishly when confronted by Afghan bandits*.

Such physical confidence is something we all have deep within, but our comfortable, predictable lives breeds it out of us. This can be regenerated. **Take your time and walk along that fallen tree trunk at the side of the path, step along those low dry rocks on the beach, get used to trusting the body-brain miracle when in awkward social situations. Know that behind your various personae, your senses are alert, that sinking into them takes your attention beyond your fretting ego-games, which unbalance you, and into a realm far more rewarding - your naturally awake physical self.**

Trust that this enables you to be alive, to live, enabling you to glide upon the cusp of this very moment when ever you choose....

* Recounted in my forthcoming autobiography.

Roadside flowers decorate the distant Picos d'Europa.
Along the Camino de Santiago, Northern Spain.

d

SELF BELIEF

This is subtly different from physical trust. Grappling with the turbulence of our demanding lives, we can lose contact with whom we have become and forget to let our brains remind us. Doing so produces surprising results.

Sometimes amongst outwardly confident people, say at a party where I know nobody, I can find myself withering, assuming they are more interesting or better than I. This affects my interactions, hearing myself speaking I feel idiotic, I wonder if my smile is genuine. The result is awkwardness, it seems people sense this and move away, redoubling my inner turmoil. Catching myself before I sink, I slip off and concentrate on the physicality of sipping a drink whilst enjoying my posture and sensual world. Soon the awareness that I am OK, that each of us has something we are good at, be it baking cakes or caring for others, arises within. I smile, at those people, at me, at life's little games. In no hurry, I let serendipity define the immediate future. Somehow, this seems to work.

As you walk, relax your mind, let go of the pressure to dance to society's tune, settle into 'you'. Sleep the night confident that your subconscious could find the solution you seek, as might taking your problems on a walk. If you can't sleep deeply, try walking around your dark home or garden, this will unwind you and prepare you for sleep. It is about believing in your astounding brain-mind's silent sorting system.

. . . talking of climbs we've done .

Christian, a brilliant yet humble French climber at the top of his game who inspired self belief up 1,000 vertical metres of terrifying granite called Le Point de l'Observatoire, in Le Parc de la Vanoise, the French Alps.

'WE'

After today's walk, **peer in the mirror and let your face twist into all sorts of silly shapes and laugh at yourself.** Who are you in any case? The walker unwinding by fooling about, the well presented character you'll return to being once at work, the private person only your family knows, or something else?

'We', as we perceive ourselves, is a cluster of assumptions and attitudes formed as our ape-minds grappled with gradually becoming a human child, as we dealt with baffling relationships. As 8 year olds we struggled with rationality, as tetchy teenagers we fought hormonal changes. We became young-adults twirling in society's shifting sands, adapting to work's weird theatres. Add on all the delicate social jigs mature adults get knotted in. Each of these inter-twined personae jostles for attention, each shouts, 'It's Me, Me, Me!'.

We are fabricated, not set in stone. We keep shifting shape as life buffets us about. Being malleable means we can make the better aspects of ourselves grow dominant. **Each time the less desired grumpy four year old manifests, smile, give them a bonbon and return to the more attractive aspects of your persona which you are presently clustering together into a complex fresh mindset.**

As you become more self-aware, you will notice a faint part of yourself silently watching these little characters pirouette. This is your attention, an element of consciousness residing in the primitive brain. This observer is untainted by the layers of reptilian, mammalian, ape and human personality. Spending time being aware of this elusive, arcane observer grants a calming security. But even *this* isn't 'You', you are all this as well as the messy rest, **so enjoy it uncritically**.

Fishermen being who they are, cooling in the sea breeze.
Feydu Island, Shaviyani Atoll, The Maldives.

DAY DREAMING

Whiling away the hour leaning on a country gate, an old codger with a straw in his mouth taking in the view. Not an exemplary image for this age, you might think, but consider this. Short, grounded bursts of daydreaming are encouraged at certain leading universities. Research shows that students who daydream, more easily absorb complex information in lectures than those concentrating on the logicality of the data being presented.

We adults are driven by pre-set ideas and conditioned logic which necessarily keeps our views stable, thus enabling us to apply known knowledge. A child's inherent purpose is to become a skilled adult, but because their minds are open, they sift through new information with ease, exploring the intriguing links between different mindsets. This too is true of scientists, inventors, innovators, creators. Plasticity is intelligence plus, plus. Allowing the mind to wander around and above reason, rather be fixated by the topic in hand, enables the 'under-mind' to learn more easily.

From time to time during your walk, lean against that lamp-post or gate, sit upon that rock or wall and let your attention wander aimlessly around the scene before you. Each time you find yourself fixing on things internal or external, unleash your attention and drift with whatever presents itself.

Once, upon Wall Street NYC, frazzled by the city's hectic activity, grounded-daydreaming unwound my tortured mind. Enjoy bursts of daydreaming, it will do wonders to your psyche. It opens you up, it lets in influences from outside, it enables you to see things in an entirely new light. It can even revive the hidden inventor-creator inside!

Amorphous by a gate, Somerset, England.

NOTHING

Now here's a challenge.

Can you stop walking and do nothing? I don't mean daydreaming, enjoying the view, pondering life's great wonders, I mean nothing. You might wonder what nothing is, if being spaced-out isn't.

A Harvard study found that 47% of the time the most attentive of us are hardly aware of the world we inhabit - we are lost in thought. Couple this to other research which shows most of us are frequently ill at ease, anxious even. There is a link.

Nothing in this sense is something you have occasionally experienced. Turning a corner, confronted by something new and extraordinary flips you into a state of simple awareness. Awed, you disconnect momentarily from your mind's emotions and thoughts; stilled, your brain is brightly alert to the novelty before you. We are not alone in this, unexpectedly coming across waterfalls, apes dance with joy. You are attentive, present, uncomplicated, balanced. Vibrantly awake. A subtle, expansive but calm static pervades, things are just so. You **linger, observing life's buzz**.

This elusive mindset often called **The Flow** can also descend upon us during or after an activity. Resting after walking up a steep incline, hesitating whilst digging the garden, pausing in the middle of an experiment, lifting your 'pen' mid sentence.

Athletes aim to capture it, for in this state of **Flow** your faculties harmonise. Think Hussain Bolt. We are aware of the primal 'Me' factor. When it next happens, linger, enjoy it, realise how lucky you are.

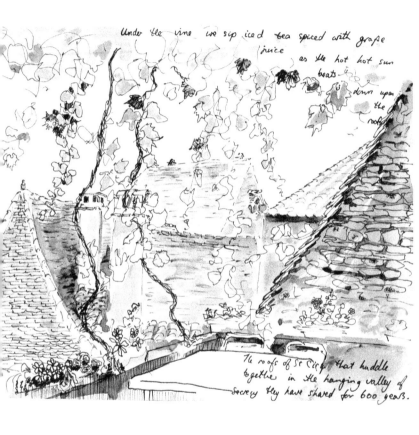

Under the vine we sip iced tea spiced with grape juice as the hot hot sun beats down upon the roofs

The roofs of St Cirq that huddle together in the hanging valley of secrecy they have shared for 600 years.

Doing nothing after sketching the view from a cafe in the Lot, France.

d

asGOODasitGETS

This moment is as good as it gets.
There is no other,
the last has gone,
the next is yet to appear.
Treasure it for what it is.
Simple as this is, it is the secret to a happy life.

You come across something interesting, don't move on as we generally do but dilly-dally. Rather than photo-snap it, **imagine you are a great artist studying the item**. Sniff the air, balance yourself, allow those inner bears to slow down. It might be a reflection upon a shop window, the arty curve of a branch, a view reaching over twenty valleys.

Before the faint awe inside flits away, savour it. Ah, what delights there are when we give them time. **Amble your mind across what you see, enjoy it easing aside your thoughts.**

A 'spark' might open inside, **smile at it, let it flood from your heart. Touch your heart with your hand, recalling touch's effect on us.** Such inner generosity creates an expansiveness, and you have the choice to develop this into a link with things beyond you.

When one of your personality traits inevitably invades with its lines of thought, do as all great folk do - chuckle, **give this fleeting persona who seeks attention a cup of tea** and return to the more profound welling within.

This is the art of living.

Of lollygaging!

An as good-as-it-gets wall made from cleanly sliced chunks of granite filled with chips. Galicia, Spain.

d

MOMENTS

Hone your awareness by slowing down and quickly writing a few snapshots of life. Here are a few rough examples from my various notebooks.

My bare toes meet the dew, crushing my weight into the cool grass this first summer's morning.

Sunlight burst through the racing clouds, illuminating droplets shaken from the rain soaked trees in the park.

Leaves crunch as I walk through the autumnal forest.

Rounding the thick oak, musty mushrooms twitch my nose.

Struck by the rising sun, rooftops create an abstract my mind flits over.

Sheltered from the swirling wind, my sun warmed skin glows.

Proud against the clear summer sky, lacy leaves sculpted by hungry caterpillars.

Water sprites whip salt from the harbour's smooth surface as fishing boats escape the storm.

Write your own observations of fleeting moments on P162-67.

There must be a shoal of small fish out amongst the moored sailing craft as a swarm of seagulls has turned the river almost black in places. Their noise dominates, drowning out the soft sounds of traffic that cross Dartbridge.

A shoal of sprats that has come in and out with the tide over the past two weeks is being chased by a shoal of mackrel and the seagulls are picking off the confused finger sized sprats. Every so often there is a wild confusion of wings as the gulls clamour to get in closer to a cluster of fish.

Observations as I sketched the River Dart, Devon, England.

WONDER

"The kind of reflection needed for poetry (ie, thinking hard about what I really feel or mean to say) is quite enough to calm my spirits." Patrick Early, poet.

The wind rages that oak, swishes the pine, roars the ash, and poplars weren't called singing trees by French peasants for nothing. Distill what you see and feel into a few mood-provoking words, (there's space on Ps162-167). Here are two fine examples to help you: my friend Patrick's work has freedom, however, should you want formality, Haikus demand three lines of 5/7/5 syllables.

Basho, the master of Haiku, wrote
(the 5/7/5 rule is lost in translation):

> The old pond,
> A frog jumps in.
> Plop!

I love the start of 'Ice Flowers' by Patrick Early:

> A freeze so pitiless it padlocks
> Everything in its tracks -
> I swing my walking stick
>
> And crack a puddle's frozen face

Loose flakes of
white cliff,

Through heat haze
silently slip;

Turning into gulls

...omptu words by the
...et David Dawson.

Together lazing, sniffing sea spray,
rapidly creating poems, swiftly
sketching during a languid
walking holiday.
Durdle Door, Dorset, England.

TRUST
...the flash-awareness...

As you move along the path, peer at yourself and get into the habit of admiring the persona you inhabit right in this moment as well as those other inner beings jostling for attention. None of these are you in total, but each are aspects of your past playing out their games. Trust this complex, subtle being you have become

and...

SMILE.*

for you are an interesting creature.

Write down potent words which define yourself right here in this specific environment (use P162-7). Slip back a bit, catch those other beings hoping to jump forward. Roll them around your brain, letting them play with each other as they paint your picture ... but make each observation brief, understanding that getting too involved locks you into that very small aspect of yourself. Did you notice that beneath the muck and muddle lies a subtle depth and strength?

Trust that, whatever is happening, this really could be a great moment to be you. Stop, relax and **Settle** (P35), gently daydreaming your way to a nothingness which is balanced, in the flow, and full of power. After this flash-awareness, slip back to your walk and be grateful you can move away.

Regardless of where or who you are, this is a soothing and strong way to inhabit your being.

---

* See the smile video-link on P168

At the eastern end of the French Pyrenees enticing walks encircle this crumbling castle above Collioure. Drawing the scene settled me to trust myself, for I was riddled with complex emotion as my utterances and actions were being professionally filmed.

GAIT

Our easy gait and ability to sweat enable us to outrun any other creature. Bushmen in southern Africa bound after prey for eight hours, occasionally hesitating to sip water. I knew tribesmen in Kenya who loped 40 miles on a Friday evening to visit distant relatives, and at dawn on Monday, jogged back to work.

Before the age of vehicles, we walked everywhere, in many countries children still walk miles to and from school. Today, most of us tire after walking two to four hours for we spend too long inactive. Oops, I'd better rise from this chair and stand whilst writing.

Savour your outstanding human body, feeling your chimp toes flexing within your shoes, your snake spine curving, those awesome legs swinging. Remind yourself of your luck, there are those who can't walk and many who can only walk short distances (I'm now one of these)**. With those sensational legs, you can travel all day long, occasionally stopping to refresh yourself.**

If you can, plan a long distance walk every so often, be it five, fifty or five hundred miles. Train by gently increasing your distance each week. I used to prepare for my Himalayan treks by mounting my stairs 100x in the morning and evening wearing my 44kg pack. At first training is difficult, but within the week you'll improve.

The longer the walk, the more it transforms the mind, which is thus able to relax. If you can't relax, it's merely a physical exercise, mentally you'll be roughly the same at the end. If you use the tricks herein, you'll find it a life-changing event. My wife certainly did over her 600 mile trek across Northern Spain.

un
cider)
te
u
good
ass by!

Legs no longer swinging, we swigged cider during a week's cycling, which is walking on a chain. Normandy, France.

℮

INCLINES

Being truly alive means being aware of your totality, which includes your health. Increasing effort pumps the heart so don't shy from using the stairs, enjoy the slope ahead, indeed, seek out steep inclines. Inclines keep us alive - statistically, those on hills live longer, slopes challenge our muscles and keep us going. People who move to bungalows on the level next to the shops are quietly killing themselves.

Hills and rises not only stimulate our quads but exercise the imagination. Apes generally stay in a single habitat, but our legs enabled us to rise over the ridge and find new valleys in the distance. **As you rise up a slope, feel your quads, your largest muscle group, extending with each step from your exquisite knees, flexing the hip which prevents us from tipping. And admire your humble kneecap - it acts as a fulcrum, greatly improving the power of the quads anchored to it.** The quads give us the best workout. If you wish, do 2x10 squats* during each walk, and if you are keen to be 'proper-fit', do so every ten minutes.

* When squatting, start gently and keep your back straight. Lower your self a little, increasing this dipping as your muscles improve. Look up how to do this safely. Even those who find walking tough can enhance their muscles, hence their physical and mental health with 30 squats daily.

Not easy steps to exercise upon, but emerging from this door you could run past those two people by that strange corner post topped with a tuft of wild grass and down to Clovelly's quayside, in Devon, England.

MINI PALS

You assume you are swinging those legs up the slope as a single being made up of the body-brain we've been exploring. Sorry to disappoint you, but this supposedly solid beast you inhabit is accompanied by bogglingly complex communities of minute, interdependent creatures.

Take your arm, where a flourishing ecosystem of micro-organisms live amongst a range of mites which clear up your dead skin. Even on the cleanest of us, bacteria galore happily defend us from other nasties. *Oh dear, itch, itch, scratch, scratch.*

At 8m long, the gut is our largest ecological environment and sensory organ. It is your main line of defence against the outside word and is where your immune system is helped by self-governing microbiota which have been developing alongside us since life began. And consider this - 90% of gut-brain nerves take messages to the brain, not from it, telling it how our immune system is doing. This raises the question, how much are we ruled by our gut or by our brain?

As you enjoy your picnic upon your various walks, thank your intelligent gut by feeding your multitudes of inner friends with food devoid of chemicals and additives. This will help you walk more fluidly. Upon regular six-week Himalayan treks, my diet was whole-wheat flour, dried vegetables, fruit and nuts, supplemented by dollops of curry and homemade yoghurt served in the rare tea stall I passed.

You are a walking continent cruising your corner of the world. Be happy that you are not as lonely as you presumed.

Horses fill their gut beneath nature's granite sculptures which enliven the coastal path stretching west from San Vincente do Grove, Galicia, Spain.

WILL

It is normal on a long walk to struggle and not find the will power to continue.

Still four more hours to the vast ridge top as I traced the wild Pindari River within which whole uprooted trees twirled past. The wide dirt track ended where a smaller river cascaded into the abandoned fury and I took a steep bridle path up which loaded mules slowly plodded. For two weeks, I'd lugged 44 kgs of winter gear, a change of clothes, rope, maps, two A4 sketchbooks, tent, cooking equipment and one month's dried food.

I'd been walking since early morning, the sun was dipping, I had to set up my tent before nightfall's heavy frosts. The way became so steep that stepping upwards needed extra will. Settling my mind on humming, the lifting of my feet and the rhythm of my heavy breathing, I plodded upwards. As concentration intensified, my pounding heart eased, my legs relaxed. I eventually reached the ridge and rang in the gods with a brass bell suspended from a tree. Before setting up my tent, I ate several buns with warming tea in a tea shack. After showering in a freezing stream, I took my evening meal at that welcome stall. I slept soundly in the frozen air, glad my mindful leg-swing had got me to the last settlement beneath the savage steppes and terrifying Himalayan peaks.

Ease the pain of exercise by relaxing and releasing your attention from it - sing, hum, follow your legs or dissect the scene unfolding before you.

old, old
-wallah.

Here he lies, in his chai-shop

awaiting the next customer. Steel-glasses washed, neatly await the next sugar sweet tea. Tin can with sugar and spoon stand expectant. Kettle gently bubbles over, sauce-pan awaits the tea-leaves, sugar, milk and water.

All is in suspension, in this ramshakle shop

As I drink tea, I sketch this typical chai shop in India's Kumaon Himalaya, I am astounded no detail has changed in the years since I'd last halted here.

PLACEBO

In want of a soporific upon a tough trek? Well, try smiling, a placebo which actually works. When you smile, you use 26 facial muscles which trick your brain into releasing neuropeptides that facilitate inter-cell communication, as well as the stress and depression killers - dopamine, endorphins and serotonin. All of this makes you feel better. Research shows that even faking it has this effect. You also look better, are taken as more reliable and amazingly, your smile makes the brains of others feel rewarded.

Think of this on today's walk ... we are responsible for the sanity of our own inner lives ... how we react determines the quality of our existence. Concentrating on a single mood intensifies it, distracting yourself from a bad one lessens it's influence, smiling (for real or fake) helps you to slide into a better mindset.

Traditional Tibetan doctors undertake surgery by inverting hot cups on the client's skin, thus taking attention from the pain of the scalpel. The ideal patient glides from their pain by imagining themselves entering a pictorial maze with a god at its centre who comes alive through total attention. This is what lies beneath the placebo effect. Interestingly, 59% of people who knowingly take a placebo pill experience less pain.

Throw your arms high and wide, SMILE and tell yourself you will make it up the mountain (at work or that Himalayan slope)! **And hum happily, thinking, "I'm OK!"** Relaxed, you see the possibility of a solution.

...les and Rosé for lunch whilst it rains outside.

A vino-placebo helping my friend and me cope with exhaustion at the long walk's end, Provence, France.

DEFINING

All creatures define their world, creating ideas which give them a short-cut to the notion behind each stimuli. Encapsulating these in various warning sounds enables group-animals to flee specific dangers without thought. Modern humans probably outstripped other human species because our rapidly developing language was based on precise description. Oddly enough, gossip also had a part. Gossip dissects relationships, illuminating who is untrustworthy. Healthy gossiping enabled cooperation, which lead to networking beyond the family or clan, hence we could create larger societies and so we outstripped other family-grouped humans such as Neanderthals. Beware, don't get addicted - named a gossip might turn you ape.

We minutely define our world, our relationships and our selves with concepts distilled into mental bombs termed 'words' and yet we are hardly aware of their power. There are hesitant words, forceful words, positive words, questioning words and more. 'Flood' makes you scuttle from the river bed and it is no folly that mantras have been used for centuries in all societies. Those Kenyan runners who consistently win Olympic medals generally come from the Kalengin peoples. When this tribal group runs, they know they are *warriors, fearless, noble*. Their bombs certainly work!

Stop strolling and take a deep breath whilst allowing a positive word-bomb to slip around your mind, maybe chose *sparkle* and so find shining objects which draw your eye.

Think of somebody who irritates you, see the words which swill around your mind, find a potent one, wrap it in a good word and roll this bundle about for a minute and see what you now think of them. Every time I passed him I was flooded with a reaction to his aggressive arrogance. Not wanting this to tarnish my consciousness, I acknowledged him, found good words. To me he is no longer a threat, but a lost person.

Brimful
— butterflies
flick rainbows
from sunstirred
wings

splashing the flowers.

Upon a long walk, the poet David Dawson and and I defined
a specific moment in our own way.
Dove Valley, Derbyshire, England.

SATISFIED?

Done this walk ten thousand times? Bored? Routine can sap our mental energy, we hope for change, but people in societies which have hardly altered for centuries are, until they become aware of alternatives, generally more contented than the rest of us. Upon being aware of what's beyond their experience, many individuals want more than what they know and leave or they remain, pining for the bright lights.

And it is transitory. A person I know is deeply dissatisfied because he's convinced he's only alive when buzzing with joy. 95% of his time is dead-time, and it is spent struggling as he yearns for happiness.

And it is relative. Once, chatting in the high Alps to a cowherd, I extolled the virtues of the view and he stopped me in my tracks. To him the glistening alpine meadows provided grass and the sparkling snows above warned of the summer's brevity. Life, he assumed, was more inspiring in the city I'd escaped.

Boredom is a mindset and mindsets are interchangeable. The routine trudge to shop can become an adventure, with a fresh mind happiness can be found anywhere. Settling in to most locations can generate satisfaction. Satisfaction lasts somewhat longer than happiness, and it leads to contentment, which certainly lasts. By now you know how to generate a 'fresh mind'.

Slow down, breathe in tune with your step. Amble along pretending you were a tourist. What drives this location? What makes it different or special? Peer at the architecture you take for granted, spotting things you might have missed. Swat up on local history to enrich your walk. Listen, feel. Accept yourself, sense satisfaction, discover contentment.

Were these cows bored of chewing the same grass week in, week out high in the Asturias, Spain?

OTHERS

Are you aware of other walkers as individuals, or are they (and those you know) the backcloth to your own dramas, merely furniture you bump into or use? When you do engage, is it to bolster your own preoccupations and personality? Is it mostly one way conversations - others being audience to your own torrential thinking? Are they merely entertainment?

Creatures survive because nature favours powerful individualism, but the various species rose above brute self-oriented existence to flourish because they were social beings thriving on interaction. Yet things have gone wonky. Today's Tech world prospers on individualism, engendering a consumerism based on narcissism. This has been termed an epidemic. Basic human traits such as empathy and compassion are in retreat world-wide. We each want a strange, individualistic standard of living unrivalled even by royalty in the past. It is why we now plunge headlong towards the convoluted cliff of social, economic and environmental devastation.

Do you notice people as distinct entities, do you listen with intent, explore their views? If so, you will not be taken as the self-inflated bore mentioned above, you might even be seen as a potential friend. **Be honest with yourself and try to improve your relationships by listening and by admiring others.** Inside yourself you will feel better, for those who genuinely enjoy others have a richer life experience. Less entangled in their own messes, they have the space to glide over the moment, to enjoy serendipity.

a cat in
the Hay
at Kantebo

I drew this old hay loft unaware of other beings, but my pen
had caught a big black cat and its kittens.
Near Gotene, Sweden.

ⓔ
EMPATHY

Is your foot sore and your leg aching from all the effort today? Rather than feeling sorry for yourself, be glad you are able to walk. There are many who can't.... I've a friend whose eyesight is failing, whose feet are distorting, whose guts are failing to properly digest hence on top of the pain, they lack energy. Knowing others are worse off, she sees herself as one of life's fortunates.

Thinking of the welfare of strangers may not come naturally, but doing so enhances our lives. This flies in the face of our consumer-driven existence, but statistically, people who empathise are happier than those who are self-obsessed. Being empathetic increases endorphins, which helps to boost our immunity because this relaxes our muscles and enables the body to better repair itself during deep sleep, which empathetic people enjoy more than most.

Ease your way home, aware of the little ways which make you fortunate. Cast your eye about, thinking constructive thoughts to do with those you pass. If this feels uncomfortable, do so for just a little while, but keep doing it for as long as you are able to partake in this *'kindful'** walking lark.

* I should know better than to invent words; = empathetic mindfulness.

Identity with the ecosystem was generated in me by these pines in the bleakness of the Fjallen Mountains, Sweden. And suddenly out popped a bear and her cubs! Losing all empathy, I quickly walked away.

SELF-KINDNESS

Ever find you're chuntering at yourself up a stretch of track? Don't worry, we all do. We are trained from the start to push, override, be our own critic and constantly compare ourselves to others. As we've seen, this makes us uneasy deep within. Subtle self-doubt festers, we feel miserable, it looks as if things will be forever dim inside.

However, juxtaposing ourselves to others stops us festering in our own self-importance, and a little doubt illuminates who we actually are. Successful people see their blemishes and mistakes as instructive stepping stones. **As you stride along the path see those little irritants are amusing trifles. Turn each one upside down - "I'm so disorganised" might become "Being scatty shows I'm creative." Take visual snapshots of the world you walk through, congratulating yourself for noticing these little gems.**

To be kind to oneself is to accept what is and to trust the under-mind will find a solution, provided you give it space*. **Breathe deeply as you walk, filling your lungs and metaphorical 'heart' (yes, go on, touch it) with positive thoughts and feelings related to your amazing body and brain.** *"The most powerful relationship you will ever have is the relationship with yourself."* Steve Maraboli, behavioural scientist and author.

Pump yourself up with marvel and adoration with each step, knowing you are as good as anyone else.

"To love oneself is the beginning of a life-long romance." Wrote Oscar Wilde. Go on, be brave and love yourself! Being kind to yourself, you will become kinder to others, for, at base, we want to please and help.

---

* Daily irritated that I'm not well, fit or vital, I instinctively push myself too strongly. When I catch myself, I stop, breathe deeply, try to admire 'me' and 'fill' my body with adoration.

Being kind to myself, I stopped on a heavy day and drew whilst sipping freshly pressed pawpaw & coconut juice plucked from these very trees. Lamu island, Kenya.

HEART THROB

Thumpty thump, your ticker goes when you stride off to catch the bus. You go faster, more blood flows around your needy body and more oxygen into your straining muscles. Dear little thing, only as big as your fist but so, so important.

Your heart is an emotional boom-box. It swoons when you meet a hero, or flutters when it's somebody you fancy. It 'shivers' when you are confronted by bullies. It spins out of control when you are confronted by a crowd expecting you to give a wise speech.

It stops dead when an ice cube is slipped down the back of your neck. It thumps all too loudly in a dark room where ghosts might lurk. Listening to your heart beat is a soothing experience, after all it is you at your most you-ish. In the night when sleep has been driven away by anxiety, it thumps, but if you slip into listening to it, you'll soon be asleep.

When you were little bigger than a pea it started and it pulsates roughly 75 times per minute, or 100,000 in a day, all day, all night. What a heart! What a wonder. Working more than any other muscle, it pumps over 7,000 litres a day around you.

And what a pistol. If you disconnect it and fired at a friend 10 metres away, you'd splash them red. Don't try this at home, unless you've a deadly sense of humour. But beware, if it has sufficient oxygen, it will beat on without you, however, if left inside, it will give one last flump as you flit to the beyond.

The ideal rock song synchs to the heart so allow it's snappy beat to help you rise up that steep slope. Touch your dear wee heart* and feel the emotional-easing this simple little act inspires. (*see P68 & 69)

Heart pounding, I stopped to draw this rocky mountain I had just climbed and which I found far more difficult to descend. Drawing calmed me and I fell into a deep, rewarding sleep in the sunshine.

Le Rubli, Switzerland.

COMPASSION

Recline against a tree or wall, enjoy the ebb & flow of long slow breaths soothing your chest. Sense by sense, cherish being in your unbelievable body, wallowing in egoless self-admiration. Gently pat yourself on the back and feel cared for, even if it is only you who cares (others will too when you are eventually filled with egoless admiration - very different to narcism).

Conjure up the image of the person you most love. Feel your fingers against their cheek, lay your lips against their ear, whisper something, pull back, peer into their eyes as you silently find potent words defining their best attributes. Unless you are a psychopath, you ought to soon feel the warmth of tenderness welling in your chest area*.

Relish this fondness increasing & spreading along your pituitary glands and filling your entire body. If it fades a little, boost it by returning to images and words of your beloved (even if this is your cat). If any negative thoughts arise, soothe them with this affection.

Beam your overflowing warmth to somebody requiring a dose of fondness. Complete this emotional aerobics, mentally hugging the one you love, yourself and this third person in a compassionate circle. If you feel strong, spread this tenderness to somebody you find disagreeable, replenishing your wellbeing when necessary. *Research shows this compassionate exercise is, incredibly, perhaps the most powerful self-healing thing you can do.*

☆

* MRI scans show emotion primarily acts upon 3 areas, the gut, heart and brain.
** If you have nobody, not even a cat, softly stroking the back your neck and heart-area fools the body into generating emotional warmth.

Compassion prompted hotel workers to stay and help tourists, rather than flee and tend to their own families when a tsunami hit Thailand's coastal resorts. Drawn from my room. Thailand.

○ ○ ○

WALKING LIGHTLY

What would you like your legacy to be? The big house your children will squabble over? A book you wrote, that much praised painting, the kindness you showed others? How about this - walk lightly through tall grass, mindful of not crushing the flowers, understanding that in this 21st century madness we must each become custodians of nature. Even the woodlice we hardly notice are affected by our passage or meddling. What a legacy it would be to leave them be.

In communist China most creatures were considered a pest - swallows, flies, mice, insects, almost anything was killed in their millions. Today this mindset lingers, a lone lizard crossing a wall is chased.

Even slugs have as much right to exist as we do, perhaps more, for unlike us they can't devastate the environment because hungry hedgehogs control them. But these are dying out because we protect badgers who've thus multiplied and are killing off our hedgehog communities. Regardless of our views, they have each existed longer than humanity and what we do now affects their future. Without comprehending this, we are alone, cold, calculating; by doing so, we are connected. This inspires concerned understanding. We learn to care, which generates empathy, happiness, a fuller life.

Compassion for others and the environment augments our experience of each walk, be it from the bedroom to the garden, the house to the office or over the hills and far away. *Walking lightly* might seem bonkers, but the concept has made me, a man who never stuck to mountain tracks, now see paths are the best way to avoid crushing those insects and their precious environments.

Being this aware is a sound legacy.

Lightly drawing nature's abundance in a garden.
Kochi, Kerala, India.

○ ○ ○

AGE

We move through our days coping as best we can. Then suddenly we are past it, aged, suffering aches and pains, regretting having paid little attention to the fading gift of a fit and healthy body, if we were lucky enough to have had one in the first place. Part of a strategy for a good life is to marvel, enjoy the little things, appreciate life's abundance, *'count your blessings'*. Our mind's health depends on our attitude, our lives depend on the quality of our minds.

Yet upon growing older, our brains can lose it. Walking 45 minutes three times a week helps enormously. **As you walk, keep flitting back through your present journey, acutely recapturing moments along the way.** Remember locking the front door, or has that memory gone with the wind? Oops, did you lock it? Be amazed your brain can retain so many memories, some 98 year olds recall detail from decades before as well as recent conversations. By doing this exercise as much as we can we ignite links between synapses, thus strengthening the mind's structure. Just before you fall asleep each night speed over your day. It is argued that such cognitive training might help deter Alzheimer's*.

It seems trite to implore we respect life, but we don't really and that is why the greatest mass extinction ever is underway. Marvelling at the world's treasures, we enhance our days in countless ways, for respect entails understanding, which engenders empathy, whose virtues we have already discussed. We can choose to live closed existences or to be open to what is around us.

*https://www.nbcnews.com/health/health-news/still-no-prevention-alzheimer-s-three-actions-can-fight-memory-n775526

Abundant life, the market town Bhowali, Kumoan Himalaya, India.

○ ○ ○

RESILIENCE

It might be a cold morning, but you have to walk (to work?). As you speed along, warm yourself by thinking deeply of your breathtaking body's resilience, regardless of what you've thrown at it, it continues and you hope it will continue to do so. You can improve your health and there are certain things we need to live a healthy life. Equanimity is the basis, so ensure you sleep well, as is frequent exercise, (but over-exercising is detrimental) and eating whole-foods. Engage in stimulating mental activity, be creative in some way, socialise… and relax.

Most studies on health and longevity have found that working for the good of others or the environment is a boost. Better to do so with other people, for socialising, having fun, laughing, is important. In my condition, socialising unfortunately exhausts me, so I try to work for the good of others by writing. Oh, and admire your stunning self.

We need a space however small, a haven where we'll be undisturbed at specific times and *be* 'me'. (I've used a broom cupboard, a toilet, a chair in the corner of a room). Though walking attentively may have become that space, we need to be utterly still for 3-5minutes each day*. Cats do, dogs do, so why not you?

'Settling' into the self, finding brightness, compassion, and residing there for a few minutes builds mental, emotional and physical resilience.

* See P156

...mbretta motorbike, a small pond and plants. A front garden beaming brightness ...eryone upon an incredibly busy road, Chiang Mai, Thailand.

○ ○ ○

TIME

Time slides between each step with a tick more regular than a grandfather clock. Life's tragedy is that we recall how it was, rarely register how it *IS*. Our moving toes scribe an arc depicting the flying present, a precious gem of irreplaceable time hardly valued as we flit between thoughts, emotions, sensations and stimuli. Our moving heel hangs in the air, leaving the present as a muddy footprint.

Gone.
In an instant the future looms.

But there is hope.
We have plastic brains,
we can surf the
cusp of the
NOW.

Upon leaving the past, lag upon this peak of the present as often as you can, momentarily hesitating, letting your foot hold time. Appreciate its fleeting magic. Stamp your heel onto it, engraining NOW in your life.

Rock your foot over this very instant!
Swish your toes across it, striding the split second
when everything happens.

Settle, with a gentle delight, knowing this is your unique
moment on life's fleeting stage.

Relish this pure sorcery before it slips into infinity.

Attentive to the present, link your best chums - your body, senses, emotions and thoughts to HERE. With gusto grasp the totality of you in a flash. Slowly but surely this develops a sense of belonging.

When you belong to the NOW, everything changes.

Time ripened cherries, Provence, France.

As with all good things, reshaping the brain's
memory structure takes practice.
You'll need to put in over 66 consecutive days,
or nothing lasting will occur.

Such practice establishes

"A pathway of kind attention,"

Says Dr Shauna Shapiro,
a leading neuroscientist.

Here are some exercises to be enjoyed on a regular basis. It's a pick and mix list, so do what suits you.

✠✠

YOGIC WALKING

Once, relaxing upon Plymouth Hoe, a friend and I were astounded when a troop of crack Special Service soldiers stopped running, laid down their guns, removed their packs and began yoga exercises. At the time I did yoga with the English cycling team's yoga teacher. Exercises such as yoga not only loosen us, but if practiced slowly and attentively, they calm us. However, attempting yogic postures as you stride to work, you'll entertain your fellow commuters as your legs get in a moving twist.

A one hour class consumes so much of our busy days... but try 3, 5 or 10 minutes of simple yogic stretches each evening before your shower*. Perform the poses with compassionate attention, delighting in every little movement. This is great exercise as well as a moving-meditation. Add in the awareness - "Amazing little body, thank you!" and your positively ignited brain will flood dopamine through your limbs, and you could be in The Flow...

Once yoga has become a habit, you could try **gently** stretching your limbs, back and neck as you walk and breathe deeply in rhythm with your slowed step.

* We are looser in the evening. Watch those 2 video-links on P169.

Winter is near - the two trees are casting leaves. I had to stop and buy myself a second hand denim jacket as the wind got cold.

Careful not to get yoga-knotted as she steps down to Totnes market, Devon, England.

✤✤
SENSUAL WALKING

Regular walkers know that after a while you can become lost within your senses, slowly dislocated from thought and emotion, noticing the detail defining your locale. Bit by bit you shift from the ghostly mind into the practical brain and reside in your body. Immersed in such silent moments, my wife's recall of her 600 mile walk across northern Spain is vivid, detailed, but not so during those moments she talked with her companion.

It is soothing and instructive to occasionally become acutely aware of this process. The mind's job is to assess, to judge, to plot, to generate action; the brain's task is to keep everything automatic going, condensing habitual acts into quick-chains which enable that action. Hey presto, we rise from the sofa for a drink.

The classic exercise on the following double-page enables you to become acutely aware of these mind-blowing actions we perform.

Sublime sensual,
Dorset, England.

⚜ ⚜

GHOST WALKING

Here is something inspiring to do, preferably not on the prow
of a boat, nor when others are watching for they might call the
doctor.

Stand still, feel gravity working on you. Take a leisurely deep
breath and stay with the tension of holding it inside. Let it out
steadily, aware of its passage up your throat, across the roof of
your mouth, through your nostrils.
Maintaining this even breathing rhythm,
very slowly, as if you were a cartoon character, lift one foot.
Feel the complex of muscles working together - around your
foot, up your leg, across your bottom, over your back.

Feel yourself unbalance as your toes reach forwards, watch
your body adjust itself. How astonishing those various
muscles, tendons, bones, sinews and cells working together to
prevent you toppling and making a fool of yourself!

Notice the bewildering engineering at work as the foot lowers,
settles, contracts as you carefully set your foot down. Which
part settled first? Heel, toes, centre?
Sense the responses in your pelvis and back as your weight
shifts, as your leg settles. Notice the foot absorbing your
weight.

Perceive bit by bit, all the interlinked actions.
Note the body momentarily relaxing.
Sense your other side reacting as the following step starts,
flicks, enacts, lands, settles.

This is sheer engineering magic. Scientists and engineers still
can't replicate such elegance. Gloat over what you are doing.
In these few seconds you've sprung from super-ape to
superhuman, for to be fleetingly aware is to be supersonic.
Well done!
Smile.

Ghost-rocking, or balancing upon a swaying boat, whilst entering Funadhu's dangerous reef. Shaviyani Atoll, The Maldives.

✠ ✠
AT HOME

Before rising from those bedsheets each morning, take a moment to flow your attention through your staggering body, from those balancing toes to the tip of your nose, relishing the privilege of inhabiting one of the known-universe's most phenomenal creations.

Rise slowly, move to the bathroom with grace, wash calmly, efficiently, attentive to sculptural you! Smile at the mirror, greeting compassionately the collection of fragile, amusing personae grinning back. Walk tall, owning yourself and your home and fill the kettle, appreciating the water's pitter-patter. If you have an outside space, whilst the water boils, stretch high and out, breathing deeply.

Enjoy greeting the plants, insects and birds with whom you share your immediate environment. Examine what the sky is about to deliver, study the quality of light beaming upon you - wondrous you! *

Occasionally withdraw from the minutiae of your day to briefly marvel at a tiny detail of existence - the ring in her voice; a sudden shift in light; the feeling of that curve of concrete. Every day set aside three minutes to do only this. Every week, six minutes wallow in the clear zone. Every month treat yourself to fifteen.

How brilliant life!
Relish as much of it as you can, for your time here really is shorter than you imagine.

* Even suffering aches & pains all the time, I do all this daily.

Maybe take up drawing outside?
*At home for 30 minutes, I calmly drew Porth Clais, whislt
walking Pembrokeshire's superb coast. Wales, Britain.*

✛✛

THREE DAY CYCLE
(ideally to be done every week for the rest of your days)

DAY ONE

A two minute Ghost Walks on your first and last steps to and from the bathroom in the morning and at night.

DAY TWO

Choose a brief activity which involves no thinking. This could be cleaning your shoes, Yoga, even doodling*. Perform this activity very, very slowly, as if you were under water (you may breathe though). Be acutely aware of the movement of each limb, digit and muscle. Watch yourself as if performing in a video instructing aliens how to be human; & SMILE!

DAY THREE

See the face of the person closest to you and love them intensely, recalling positive things about them. Sense your *'heart-strings'* singing and linger. After a while, spread this warmth to a friend. Then, out in the world, spill it over to the shopkeeper (yes, just do it, but unobtrusively or they'll call the cops). Now flood that emotion all over somebody who annoys you. Finally, waft it back to yourself.

DAY 4 (maybe a Sunday?)

"It's a 3 day cycle!" You say. Like to live better? "Yes!"

For 10-15-20 minutes at most, it is potent to combine Days **1,2&3** on day **4** - in any order you like. One day add on the 5 minute sitting session on P156.

---

* *Which is why I developed my calm-doodle book 'Settling'.*

On looking

closer,

there are

two—

REVIVING EXERCISE ✆

We need exercise and doing this 2-4 minute gem will help you stay fit! It is good when you are not able to walk due to time pressure or when recovering from sickness but pine to do a little something. Combining 6 undemanding routines, it works most muscles in your body provided you gently **tense** them as you move. Don't over-swing, listen with intent to the messages your body is sending out. Be attentive throughout to enhance the effect.

If fit, do each stage 10-15 times (if not, 2-5x). Ideally, do this cycle morning, noon and evening. It will take a few attempts to engrain the process, but it is worth it.

Stand tall.
Have a flash-awareness of your body, senses and mood.
Gently **tense** your muscles.

1. Keeping your arms straight, swing them **sideways** from thighs to far above your head and back down.
2. Swing arms together **forwards** from just behind the thighs to high above your head & back down.
3. Arms to front, **twist** your torso fully left, right.
4. Arms dropped, bend your torso **sideways** left, right.
5. Arms up to front, back-straight, **squat down,** rising.
6. Lift each **knee** up and down.

Relax deeply as oxygen rushes through you. Your body will continue 'working' for 3-4 hours afterwards.

Smile.
This and the attentiveness have done you good.

Busy in Cherbourg's fishing harbour, France.

SO WHY SITTING?

SO WHY SITTING?

Although this book is packed with it, I have avoided that strange word 'mindfulness' because it is riddled with twenty-five centuries of confusion. Research shows that we interpret stimuli in a manner which syncs with, and reinforces our engrained views and hunches. Think tribalism, cultism, racism. Critical thinking makes us less likely to get lost in such common mental cul-de-sacs of self-delusion.

However, in meditational circles discriminatory thought can mistakenly be taken as a negative encumbrance. This attitude hinders the mind's reality-monitoring, thus impairing intellectual accuracy, inviting misinterpretations, distorting memories. Such cloying conditioning makes us become more of what we were or what we want, and, crucially, detached from what is. This is problematical - few of us have matured beyond emotions formed by our fifth birthday. Hmm. Yet we can avoid being stuck up our own ego, ie, very *conscious* but none-the-less *lost in o0urselves*.

Alert awareness brightened by candid self-observation leads to a more open attitude, producing a collaborative mind which is engaged, not detached. Such engagement generates empathy, increasing compassion and openness, helping to generate longer telomeres, thus slowing ageing. And research indicates that quiet meditation thickens the structure of our brains: amazingly, 50 year old brains of (such open) meditators resembled those of 30 year olds who didn't[o]. Caring transmutes us:- caring for ourselves, for others, for our environment.

The micro-boosts herein, unencumbered by philosophical riddles, underwritten by research, deliver the effect of formal meditation. Yet sitting quietly for short periods each day 'practising' attentiveness and compassion consolidates the effect*, adding extra potency.

---

* Something Britain's National Health Service wishes we all did.

[o] 18 months after a well monitored stroke, MRI scans showed my brain to be 20+ years younger than my physical age, boggling two cerebral consultants.

Wearily setting down my pack during a six week solo Himalayan trek, drawing this tiny temple into which you could only crawl, made me mindful, or calmly aware, of my surroundings.

5 - 10 Mins SITTING

Be assured, this exercise is more effective and captivating than counting your breath! And there's little to it. As you have discovered thus far, being spellbound by your entirety is an engaging thrill. You relate to what's around you, you gain sincerity, hence concern, and thus compassion. And things simply get easier.

Residing at the cusp of our mental/emotional frontiers, at our interface with the world, sensual input is interpreted more cleanly, we decide to act conscious of a universal, rather than a selfish vantage.

Should you feel sitting is a daffy-dippy activity, consider that they do it in Silicon Valley, as do crack troops*.

Enter your secret little haven,
close the door on life's stresses.
There is no need for incense or cross-legged knots.

Stand tall, legs spread wide, arms raised high and
breathe slowly, deeply, regaining a sense of being in a
body-brain
rather than stuck in
a mind.

Once hooked, edge in the odd extra minute until you reach your happy zone. You might increase to the minimum daily 10mins scientists recommend for better health.

*Attention alone can be hard, ego-bound, narrow; empathy softens, enlightens, opens.

sitting

Slowly sit down.
Feel gravity at work.
Eyes open.
Notice the temperature on your sensational skin.

Flow with the movements your breath creates, thanking
this natural process for keeping you alive.

Be enthralled by every bit of your structure from your
ears to your ankles and appreciate the fascinating little
things your body is up to whilst you happily sit there.

Relish the stellar creature you are, admiring details of
your 3 billion year development.

Sensually admire the space around you.

Close your eyes,
delight in somebody you love.
Reside in this compassionate warmth.

Smile at this weird and wondrous life and well with
rapture.

How wonderful to be alive,
to feel like this.

Keep telling yourself that what you are currently doing
adds value to your existence.

a gem
(for those times when discretion is required)

Stand or sit tall & settle into where you are *(taking only a few seconds)*. Enjoy this activity whilst suffusing yourself with kindness.

Breathe in energising oxygen.

Hold this living ball bright in your mind.

Let it out,
relaxing your remarkable being.

Smile.

Though simple, if done with attention, this exercise incorporates much of what we have been doing in this book. Raw sensual awareness, visualisation of a natural process, appreciation of your totality, joy. And more... Repeated inconspicuously anywhere, as you walk, work, talk, even when in pain, it can fill you with positivity. Eventually the process is engrained, you will Flow. Dislocated from an ego-driven, tribal orientation, you will stand clear, refreshed, revived - as your 'self'.

To cope with deep, constant pain everywhere, and to prepare for this medical condition's inevitable brain-suppression, (and subsequent depression), I developed this self-loving technique for myself.

The head of La Vallee D'Aspe, French Pyrenees.

ENDING

Throughout this little book we have hopefully been walking the walk, together in step and attitude, quietly attentive to what life gives us. Awareness of this moment's subtle treasures, however fleeting, reinforces the strong, poised mindset we have developed over these weeks or months. Open to what is around us, we are released from being glued to a host of unwanted inner complexes.

Self-aware, self-empathetic, released from society's judgemental traps, we move of our own volition in this calm, composed and compassionate state. Aware we are connected to everything, however microscopically, our inner lives are vastly enriched.

We need little more.

Every season presents a myriad of inspiring little theatres to enrich our walks. Notice the makeup of the sky, how this alters the light falling on and around you. Listen to the orchestra of sounds. Smell and breathe deeply.

Cast your eye about, seeking secret dens, webs, paths. Know you are a magnificent little planet, sense you are a part of the delicate eco-systems surrounding you.

Ha! The interconnectedness of everything.

Stepping from your little puddle,
you experience a flash-awareness of your total self,
Over and over again.

Precariously!!
Between the sea thrift and surf
Just a kestrel's mew

*Haiku by David Dawson as we lazed upon
Dorset's Jurassic Cliffs, England.*

REFERENCES.

Still in doubt, tempted to throw this book across the valley? Peek at a tiny bit of the research underscoring it's pages. A few examples of videos and articles of the topics covered:-

(Also as a subpage on my website iaindryden.com/books - see references beneath the advert for this book and tap on the link)

Smiling - A TED Talk (brief, inspiring videos of world experts)
- https://www.ted.com/talks/
  ron_gutman_the_hidden_power_of_smiling?language=en

Brain-changing benefits of exercise (13 mins) -
 https://www.ted.com/talks/
wendy_suzuki_the_brain_changing_benefits_of_exercise?
utm_source=tedcomshare&utm_medium=email&utm_campai
gn=tedspread

Walk!(3min) - https://www.ted.com/talks/
nilofer_merchant_got_a_meeting_take_a_walk/up-next?
language=en
(5min) - https://www.ted.com/talks/
marily_oppezzo_want_to_be_more_creative_go_for_a_walk/
up-next?language=en

Springy step (4mins) but got to 3.20 mins for info on spring. -
https://www.youtube.com/watch?v=OxUXA8xPs68

Foot's 3 arches (article + 8 min video) - http://root2being.com/
foot-shape-and-function/foot-anatomy-and-structure/

Barefeet vs shoes?(3 mins) - https://www.youtube.com/watch?
v=nz-cB0kX-lk

Balance - https://www.sharecare.com/health/types-of-exercise-
programs/why-is-balance-training-important
https://www.askdoctork.com/why-are-balance-exercises-
important as-we-age-201301114100
https://www.gaiam.com/blogs/discover/what-good-balance-
does-for-your-body-and-how-to-get-it

Stones - ted.com/talks/
amishi_jha_how_to_tame_your_wandering_mind

Taste - https://www.ted.com/talks/
heribert_watzke_the_brain_in_your_gut/up-next

Emotion (20 mins. Excellent, but perhaps ignore the advert for his App?)
- https://www.youtube.com/watch?v=h-rRgpPbR5w

Compassion...starting with an old friend's 13 minutes talk
- https://www.ted.com/talks/daniel_goleman_on_compassion/
discussion

Self-love (37 mins) - https://www.youtube.com/watch?
v=MEyJ_H1U5SQ
(19 mins) - https://www.youtube.com/watch?v=oLxoBF7lWNA

Yoga - https://www.youtube.com/watch?v=_NnTAlk2vdk
Simple yoga referred to on P108 (to be done evening or morning)
(5 mins) https://www.youtube.com/watch?v=GF67wiX9wUE
(4 mins) https://www.youtube.com/watch?v=V5BGbnVevsc
More...
https://www.youtube.com/watch?v=oLxoBF7lWNA

Mindfulness   (13 mins) - https://www.youtube.com/watch?
v=IeblJdB2-Vo
(8 mins) - https://www.youtube.com/watch?
v=m8rRzTtP7Tc&vl=en
(19 mins)- https://www.youtube.com/watch?v=1nP5oedmzkM

And more :-
-https://www.psychologytoday.com/us/blog/feeling-it/201211/
the-best-kept-secret-happiness-health-compassion
https://www.health.org.uk/blog/importance-empathy
https://www.medicaldaily.com/surprising-health-effects-
empathy-240983
https://www.sciencedirect.com/science/article/pii/
S0889159118300473
https://leightremaine.com/9-powerful-benefits-of-compassion/

You may wonder about the author's credentials.

Anyone could attempt a book about walking with attention. This thought kept arising as the information herein was tested against scientific research, during the arduous process o writing, refining, editing editing. For what it's worth, here we are:

WALKING The author has walked thousands of miles including:- chunks in Kenya; Delhi to London with transpor thrown in when necessary; dozens of Himalayan, Alpine European treks lasting weeks; his holidays revolved around walking. When osteoarthritis and ill health discouraged moving more than two hundred metres, he bought crutches so he could enjoy paths in the Pyrenees and beyond.

ART Iain Dryden's work sold in galleries and he once had a small art company in London which he gave freely to his employees when he decided to become a teacher. He is currently exploring a new painting venture.

WRITING Iain has written for Education since 1988. One of his works was serialised by the BBC, for whom he also wrote extra material. Another work gained a BBC Writing Award. He conceptualised, set up and edited an environmental magazine for Education which was held up in Parliament as exemplary. He's written environmental/geographical books, articles, material for teachers & children's stories to convey key ideas. He organised environmental education conferences, at the time unique so drawing people nationwide. He currently has several books published at - iaindryden.com/books

MEDITATION For 4 years Iain practised nothing but yogic and mindful meditation, months of which was in a secluded Himalayan house with a group of 4 including: the world renowned psychologists Dan Goleman; the ex-Harvard professor of psychology Ram Dass; the American singer Krishna Dass. Iain went on to help run and teach in London's first unaligned meditation centre, Chelsea's 'Gandalf's Garden'; put on a pedestal, he left to teach in state schools.

Iain Dryden believes the calm, awake state attained during 'mindfulness' is achieved in many ways, and that compassion and self-love are key to being a balanced character.

Ɔn a personal note, my ideal walk involves

drawing

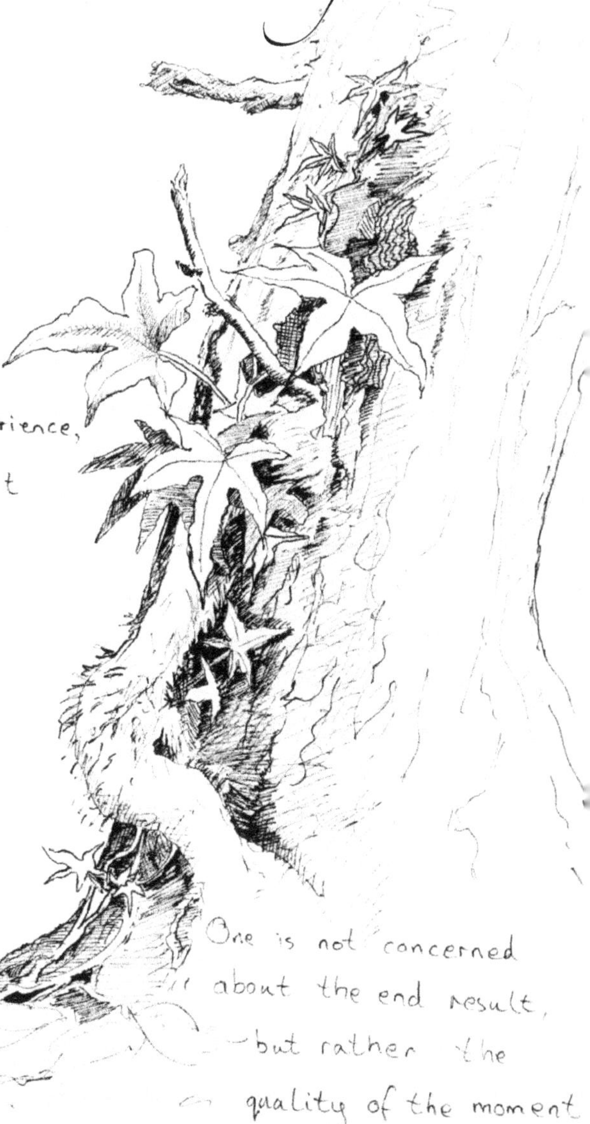

ɜv of drawing

is a

sobering experience,

one can't

be in a

hurry,

ıe has to be

the moment,

have

o desire

ther than

o

ɾdw.

One is not concerned

about the end result,

but rather the

quality of the moment

Other works by Iain Dryden
iaindryden.com

Camino Voices - Voices of long distant walkers bring to life Northern Spain's 600 mile pilgrimage, which is illustrated with Iain's pen and ink drawings.

Settling - Easy, proven exercises which help relaxation and de-stressing, using doodling as a base.

Bush Boy - A page-turning almost crazy, adventurous autobiography written as a sting of exciting, interlinked cameos across half the world.

Fiction -
Satya's Truths. *A novel.* Ewan, a stiff upper-crust English artist, flees to India after an accidental crime, only to enter a constantly unpredictable adventure which proves to become an uncalled-for quest. Three powerful women, a wise herbalist and a string of charlatans, as well as a challenging Himalayan winter, soften and open Ewan to empathy and self understanding. And possibly love.
Two other novels are in the making.

Children's stories still available -
Ice cream. A bully is thwarted upon a seaside pier.
Blow up. An adventure warning of inflatable lilos blown out to sea.
Respect. A tough lad gains his teacher's respect in a surprising way.
Mahout. A girl falls for an elephant she'd feared.
Monsoon. A boy and his father survive a storm in the Indian Ocean.
Web chat. Two girls start a campaign to stop injustice.
Lamu. A race around a Kenyan island proves to be morally instructive.

Educational works still in print.
Llandudno & Kochi. Two environmental and cultural studies, with teacher's notes and classroom work included. (an exciting sound rendition with well known actors still on **BBC** School's Radio)

thanks

Thanks to my editor in chief, Millie my wife!

&

Thanks to those who believed in this project.

Smile

Contact me or see more *iaindryden*.*com*

Font used - Optima
(sometimes Gill Sans light)
Worldwide Copyright© - Iain Dryden
registered February 2018
by iaindryden com

Published January 2020 by FeedARead.com Publishing.

A CIP catalogue record for this title is available from the British Library.